OVERCOMING
PORNOGRAPHY ADDICTION

A Spiritual Solution

J. Brian Bransfield

Cover art © by prudkov / Shutterstock.com
Cover and book design by Lynn Else

Library of Congress Cataloging-in-Publication Data

Bransfield, J. Brian.
    Overcoming pornography addiction : a spiritual solution / J. Brian Bransfield.
    pages cm
    Includes bibliographical references (pages   ).
    ISBN 978-0-8091-4797-7 (alk. paper) — ISBN 978-1-58768-082-3
1. Sex—Religious aspects—Catholic Church. 2. Catholic Church—Doctrines.
3. Internet pornography—Religious aspects—Christianity. 4. Computer sex—
Religious aspects—Christianity. 5. Catholic men—Religious life. I. Title.
    BX1795.S48B73 2013
    241'.667—dc23

                                                                2012039352

ISBN: 978-0-8091-4797-7 (Paperback)
ISBN: 978-1-58768-082-3 (E-Book)

Published by Paulist Press
997 Macarthur Boulevard
Mahwah, New Jersey 07430

www.paulistpress.com

Printed and bound in the
United States of America

TABLE OF CONTENTS

To Blessed Pope John Paul II

"Spouses are therefore the permanent reminder to the Church of what happened on the Cross; they are for one another and for the children, witnesses to the salvation in which the sacrament makes them sharers."

Familiaris consortio 13

FOREWORD

The worth of a book is to be measured by what you
can carry away from it.
Viscount James Bryce (1838–1922)

This is a very worthy book. Every reader will take away a deeper
understanding of the public health crisis of Internet pornography and an experience of how much the Lord Jesus has to offer
to those entangled in it. *Overcoming Pornography Addiction: A
Spiritual Solution* names the demon and exposes the lie. A false
promise of freedom is unmasked as a sinister form of slavery that
shackles every human person in a cell of hopelessness and
despair. Thanks be to God, this book also offers the great hope
of renewal and freedom to those who have the humility and
courage to seek healing in and from the Lord.

Msgr. Bransfield is a gifted and generous priest. In this
book it is made evident that he knows the Lord well, and he
invites us to come know him, too. The invitation to encounter
Christ in this book come from a man with a shepherd's heart and
is a great example to every disciple of what it means to be committed to the new evangelization.

Internet pornography is a monstrous industry and it threatens the inherent value of every human person, not just its producers, purveyors, and victims. Msgr. Bransfield tells a compelling
story of how this scourge of the digital revolution is a natural

devolution from the dehumanizing aspects of the industrial revolution and the sexual revolution. In response to the dark facets of this modern age, the great gift and beauty of the chaste life—for married and single persons alike—is presented as the achievable fruit of a life of virtue lived in communion with God and neighbor.

Pornography promises its users entertainment, relaxation, and fulfillment. In fact, Internet pornography has emerged as one of the single largest threats to true human freedom. By sounding the alarm, this book adds to the work of many others who seek to guide and support those who are trapped in a cycle of destructive behavior. This book is insightful and practical; it promises to be a resource for those challenged and those who seek to help.

My colleagues at Saint Luke Institute (www.sli.org) and I are actively engaged in the assessment and treatment of persons who suffer from a variety of behavioral problems and addictions, including the increasing issue of Internet pornography. We know from experience how insidious the temptation of Internet pornography is for good people. Well-meaning men and women are inextricably caught in cycles where they cease to be masters of their own decisions—Internet pornography takes their life over and threatens ruin.

To whom shall they go?

Msgr. Bransfield invites us along with him as he accompanies Jesus on his journey through Samaria. We stop at the well with the Lord where he meets the Samaritan woman who thirsts for life and more. Her life is changed forever by the encounter, and the reader's is, too.

In a compelling and kind way, Msgr. Bransfield introduces a path of forgiveness, virtue, and healing for those willing to accept the invitation to encounter Jesus. Those suffering from an out-of-control lifestyle are encouraged to toss away the manacle of shame that inevitably accompanies Internet pornography addiction.

Msgr. Bransfield tells his readers "there are no magical solutions to life." Having said this, he also reminds us that Christ performs miracles of healing every day. As someone who knows many women and men who have suffered the agony and shame of entrapment in cycles of addiction and shame, I can testify to the truth of such miracles. Quality mental health care integrated with well-grounded spiritual direction and a lifestyle of supportive love can help anyone conquer addiction. The vision of the human person revealed in our Scriptures and the teaching of the Catholic Church promise great hope to those who suffer from Internet pornography addiction.

I encourage everyone to read this book. Please accept Msgr. Bransfield's invitation to encounter Christ. It is well worth it.

Rev. Msgr. Edward J. Arsenault
President and CEO
Saint Luke Institute
Silver Spring, Maryland, USA
Louisville, Kentucky, USA
Manchester, England
Pretoria, South Africa

PREFACE

This book began when I was invited to deliver a keynote address to clergy, diocesan and parish staff, and faithful in the Archdiocese of Omaha, Nebraska, in February 2009. The Archdiocese had recently formed a wide-ranging antipornography task force, made up of specialists in various fields, and had developed a series of diocesan workshops on the topic. Mary Beth Hanus, manager of Victim Outreach and Prevention in the Archdiocese, had heard my presentation at the Promise to Protect Workshop for the United States Conference of Catholic Bishops (USCCB) the year before, and invited me to speak on the topic of Internet pornography in the archdiocese. I am very grateful to Mary Beth for the gracious invitation.

More indirectly, this book is the fruit of my studies at the Pontifical John Paul II Institute for Studies on Marriage and Family, and of my pastoral experience in the various settings of parochial ministry. The teaching of Blessed Pope John Paul II on marriage, family, and the inviolable dignity of human life is being received at a rapid pace across demographic lines and over generational chasms. One of my goals in this work was to take his overall teaching and apply it to the painful and tragic phenomenon of Internet pornography and its devastating effect on marriage, family life, and the human person. The thoughts expressed in this book are those of the author alone and do not necessarily reflect any position of the USCCB or any other institution regarding the matters discussed herein.

Dangerous contemporary trends and the dominant cultural mindset of modern relativism drain meaning and avoid mystery at all costs. What was a slippery slope in the previous generation has now become an avalanche in the current. At the center of the avalanche of secularism is the notion that human life is disposable, human sexuality is only for satisfying one's personal erotic needs, and a child is a trophy to show off rather than a gift to be treasured. Internet pornography has taken its place in the onslaught against the dignity of human life, marriage, family, human sexuality, and the child. Many people of good will have tripped, fallen, and been buried underneath the countless counterfeits of love that attempt to pass pleasure off as beauty and satisfaction as fulfillment.

The teaching of Blessed Pope John Paul II is the tectonic shift that can tilt the mountain and stem the avalanche. His teaching is not a passing fad or a movement of the moment. Rather, his teaching leads us to authentic meaning, genuine fulfillment, lasting beauty, and the treasure of mystery for which generations have long ached and often searched. This mystery and meaning are found only in Jesus Christ and his Church. The hope is this book may serve as a foothold in the avalanche. These pages are about the stability of the life of grace and virtue found only in the teaching of Christ and the ministry of his Church. Further, the hope is these pages may lend strength for one more step upward and forward, however faltering at times, through the barrage and into the true freedom of the "culture of life" and a "civilization of love." As such, this work is gladly dedicated to the memory and honor of Blessed Pope John Paul II.

I am grateful to the many people who have supported me in these efforts, most especially my archbishop, the Archbishop of Philadelphia, the Most Reverend Charles J. Chaput, OFM Cap. I also am thankful for the support of Monsignor Ronny Jenkins, USCCB General Secretary; Andy Lichtenwalner, PhD; Peter Murphy, DMin; Brian and Joan Gail; Cynthia and Martin Lutschaunig and their sons, Christian, Daniel, and Andrew; as well as my sisters and brother, Margaret Anne, Mary Jane, Paula, and Paul.

INTRODUCTION

There are no magical solutions to life. History and legend are filled with disastrous stories of unfortunate characters who have been captivated and obsessed by the quest for magical words, enchanted items, spells, charms, dust, potions, touch, or relationships. Even though the logic of science has long banished sorcerers and wizards to fantasy stories and fairy tales, we cannot dispel the shortcut appeal of magic. The search for magic is compelling because of the prospect of a tremendous amount of power located in a very minimal amount of effort. The pursuit of magic is a dangerous temptation, not because it is futile and a waste of time, but because when we search for magic, we are really looking for *power*.[1] The fact that magic is fictitious does not protect us from the very real pain that arises when we attempt to grasp power as the world defines it.

There are no magical solutions to life. The quest for magic is based in the fantasy that our whims can somehow escape reason. Although we know in our heads that magic does not exist, this message has not passed down to our hearts. Many people still attempt to find and master magical solutions to the genuine difficulties of life. At least two things happen if we try to conjure up magical responses to life: First, we become frustrated because the very wishes and illusions we attempt to summon always escape our grasp. Second, we begin to internalize an unreal way of dealing with life. When we do return to real life, our interac-

1

tions are blunted and diminished. Life becomes even more difficult. The attempt at the quick fix has made our original difficult situation worse. Inevitably, the attempt to use "magic" backfires in sinister distortion and with disastrous consequences. If we pursue the unreal, we begin to live in an illusion. If we attempt to master the unreal, we may become wounded and find ourselves in grave danger.

There are no magical solutions to life. The search for magic is very much like the preoccupation with Internet pornography. Magic purports to be instantaneous, without effort or cost, and alleges to bring about or cause exactly what we want in the moment. For many, the tapping of the keyboard amounts to a form of technological incantation to conjure forth what we believe to be a quick fix. Sexually explicit images can appear on the computer screen almost instantly, with little physical effort and apparently low financial cost, and excite the sexual urge with seemingly no commitment. But this is the curse of magic and illusion: Instead of freeing the user, Internet pornography *enslaves* the user. Instead of bringing relief, it imposes a burden. Instead of satisfying the user, it makes the user even hungrier. Instead of the vigorous promotion and protection of the sanctity of human sexuality, the user is weighed down in sins against chastity and human dignity. Instead of deepening the relation between sex and marriage, Internet pornography severs this relation, reducing sex to using the self and the image of another for pleasure. Love is excluded. The magic becomes a curse.

There are no magical solutions to life; there are only living solutions to life. This book is about living solutions. It is not about magic; it is about work. It is not about fixing our life, but about healing our wounds. It is not about satisfaction, but fulfillment. It is about the life of virtue founded upon the all-sufficient grace of Jesus Christ. The mission of the Church calls for great pastoral urgency in addressing the phenomenon of Internet pornography. The personal and social impact of the routine ability to access the World Wide Web through a home or business computer network goes beyond advertising, data transfer, research, commerce, communication, and information sharing. Despite the benefits technology may bring, it is a considerable threat to marriage and the family and therefore to culture. Technology tends to short circuit the full dimension of human experience. The intersection of the Sexual Revolution and the Digital Revolution has provided some of our oldest appetites a brand new venue: cybersex. When tempted to click on vice, we must tap instead into virtue. The only path away from the sins associated with virtual reality is real virtue.

METHODOLOGY

Healing the wounds of Internet pornography is a journey. As our guide, we will take Jesus in his meeting and conversation with the anonymous woman of Samaria. Although Jesus is our guide, he is also the destination. In him are all the treasures of grace and virtue.

Chapter 1 opens with a practical example of the power of Internet pornography and its devastating effect on men and women, and on marriage. It demonstrates how the user of pornography is cornered and caught in dangerous territory through the growing prevalence of Internet pornography.

Chapter 2 presents the necessary journey of Jesus in which he encounters the woman of Samaria who has suffered much at the hands of many men. The words of Jesus become the compass that guides those who suffer to come to the fount of healing virtue.

Chapter 3 reviews the major fault line causes, warning signs, and effects of Internet pornography use, as well as the significant challenges presented by Internet pornography and how it is different from conventional pornography.

Chapter 4 navigates the important first steps to healing including hitting bottom, examining one's conscience, understanding the occasion of sin, approaching the sacrament of reconciliation, and receiving forgiveness. This chapter also maps out the important role of a prudent spiritual director or wise counselor who can help the user identify the myth of gratification. As such, this chapter traces and highlights the crucial network of honesty, transparency, and accountability.

Chapter 5 continues the turn to healing, emphasizing the essential importance of leaning on Jesus through the action of the Holy Spirit. This chapter points out the true north of Eucharistic adoration in the life of prayer.

Chapter 6 pinpoints the teaching of Blessed Pope John Paul II, in particular on the Theology of the Body, as the course to a proper understanding of the identity of the human person. Understanding the person as a gift of self in love charts the way to the cultural foundation necessary to help transform society into a "culture of life" and a "civilization of love" through the internalization of the virtue of temperance.

THE GOAL OF THE WORK

There are no magical solutions to life, and certainly none to the problem of Internet pornography. These pages point to and do not replace or substitute for the grace of Christ that comes to the believer in and through the sacraments. This book is also not meant to replace the important resource of prudent counseling, wise spiritual direction, or helpful 12-step groups. It is not meant to substitute for consultation with one's physician or care provider. In fact, this book is best used in consultation with one's health care provider, professional counselor, and spiritual director. There are many fields of the human sciences that have already offered an understanding of the pain of Internet pornography. I do not seek to duplicate or even offer a summary of their expertise, because that is not my area of specialty. I seek to offer an understanding of the first grace-filled healing steps for one caught up in Internet pornography, and at the same time convey an understanding of the human person which will assist us to advance upon the pastoral urgency and implications that the phenomenon of Internet pornography presents to the Church. With such an understanding in place, we can then respond to this phenomenon with the more robust help of grace and the life of virtue. In this we learn, adapt, and effectively utilize the wisdom of the human sciences. This work is offered as a door to spiritual support that can advance the journey to freedom. The goal of the work is to protect human dignity and to safeguard the sanctity of human sexuality.

CHAPTER 1

THE PREVALENCE OF INTERNET PORNOGRAPHY

TOM AND NANCY

It is about 11:15 p.m. on Tuesday evening. Tom and Nancy have been married eleven years and have two school-age children.[1] They have lived in the same house for nine years, and are doing fairly well. The children have been asleep for two and a half hours. Nancy and Tom are in bed propped up on pillows, concluding their nightly ritual of reading before falling asleep. Nancy regularly turns the pages of her novel. If Nancy were watching, she would see Tom has not turned a page in more than ten minutes. She might think his mind is miles away, at the office, as he concentrates on unfinished business from work. But really, his mind is only yards away, in the den downstairs, at the computer. All he has thought of during the morning at the office, in afternoon meetings, in traffic on the way home, through dinner, and while helping the kids with their homework is that screen glowing to life. When could he be alone to get online?

He had experienced pornography during high school. He had first seen it as older teammates passed it along in the locker room snickering and joking. He has struggled with attachment to viewing pornographic magazines from time to time, but pornography had never preoccupied him like this before. Ever since the pop-up ads and spam e-mail had enticed him to follow the links, he has not been able to find a way back. Day after day, pornography is only a click away. Driving to work, he thinks curiously of sexualized words and phrases to type into the search engine. From pictures to stories, from chat rooms to streaming videos, the supply is seemingly endless. He tells himself tonight will be the last time. He tells himself he will do this just one more time, and only for fifteen minutes. The last time he logged online, he surfed from porn site to porn site for four hours. He rationalizes that tonight will actually be an improvement; he will only be on for fifteen minutes. He further rationalizes: "At least I am not out with a prostitute."

He glances over. Nancy's novel has fallen from her hands. At some point, she turned over and is fast asleep. Tom slips from under the covers, lightly steps around to the bedroom door, and turns out the light. He closes the door behind him as he moves into the hallway and to the stairs. He knows his way in the dark by now. He moves down the steps, skipping over the fifth one, which creaks. He moves into the foyer and to the den. He turns on the low-voltage desk light and clicks on the computer. His heart is racing; his eyes are wide. He sees only the screen. For the next four hours, he searches and clicks, and falls deep into the world of Internet pornography.

At about 3 a.m., Nancy awakens. She feels the emptiness across the bed. Tom is not there. She looks to the master bath—darkness fills the space beyond the open door. She slips from the bed, dons her robe, opens the door, and goes into the hallway. The children's doors are closed. She descends the stairs, and detects a faint trace of light coming from the den. She enters. Tom is sound asleep in the chair at the desk. Working again, she thinks. Do his colleagues work this intensely, until three in the morning? She moves to rouse him gently with one hand, and the other moves to bring the screen back so she can log off the computer. As he stirs, she glances at the screen.

How do you think Nancy feels? Used? Guilty? Traumatized? Betrayed? Rejected? Violated? Suspicious? She thinks, "We're married; what were you looking for?"

CORNERED AND CAUGHT: INTERNET PORNOGRAPHY

The victim is cornered, if not caught, almost before he can turn away. Because of fallen human nature and the highly visual nature of the masculine sexual drive, men are particularly at risk to fall victim to sexually explicit images on the computer screen—considerable risk. The pain of Internet pornography begins from a variety of diverse circumstances: An accidental click on an ambiguous Web address leads to a site with pornographic images; a moment of curiosity and loneliness leads a husband to type the letters of a sexual phrase or word into a search engine to see what emerges; a "recreational" or regular user of pornographic magazines feels the thrill of exploring a site with endless links, where there is no final page. A young man visits an "adult" Web site, blog, or Internet forum he has heard others talk about at the bar.

Accident, curiosity, loneliness, fantasy, apparent recreation, or hearsay: each of these circumstances can provide the glimpse that introduces the rush and paves the way to a labyrinth of temptation that promises satisfaction, but delivers dangerous frustration and sin. Even the most devoted family man and virtuous churchgoer runs a high risk and considerable vulnerability in sitting at the keyboard. The images, along with the apparent secrecy and seemingly easy entry, gain quick access to a man's most persistent drives and appetites. Regardless of his talents, gifts, skills, or potential, the cunning trap of Internet pornography outwits the clever and overwhelms the naive. The extensive patterns and destructive habits of sexually explicit images on the Internet are like a tsunami that not only erodes, but decisively overwhelms, in a matter of moments, healthy boundaries that have been in place for years. The menacing reach of Internet pornography has captured a considerable number of well-meaning men.

THE PREVALENCE OF INTERNET PORNOGRAPHY

Tom and Nancy find themselves, their marriage, and their family in the grip of an insidious phenomenon. Pornography is a twelve billion to fifteen billion dollar industry in the United States, and a fifty-seven billion dollar per year industry worldwide. The growth of the porn industry has doubled in value since 2006. Sex represents the third largest economic sector on the Internet.[2] The first is buying computers themselves, and the second is buying software. The third most searched-for word on Internet search engines is "sex." The first two are "and" and "the."[3] Video pornography takes in more annual revenue than professional baseball, football, and basketball *combined*.[4] There are more than four million pornographic Web sites. The majority of e-porn access and traffic takes place between the hours of 9 a.m. to 5 p.m. on weekdays.[5]

The three basic reasons often given for Internet pornography are gratification, validation of the needs of the intangible self, and financial profit. Promiscuous sexual gratification is the pursuit of physical indulgence without responsibility or accountability to the sanctity of human sexuality. Validation is the experience of persons who previously have not understood their sexuality in a mature manner, and who explore sexual topics through the filter of the Internet, which allows for apparently anonymous discussion with other persons. The Internet provides a screen or mask through which persons can hide and think themselves "safe" as they explore previously misunderstood or poorly understood issues of sexual feelings and inclination. Sadly, such persons have apparently never benefitted from a safe and virtuous setting in which to discuss and understand human sexuality. Instead, they have, through the Internet, found a highly unsafe and vice-filled place to discuss and explore sexuality.

CHAPTER 2

"IF YOU KNEW THE GIFT OF GOD" (JOHN 4:10)

THE NECESSARY JOURNEY OF JESUS

One day, Jesus was on a journey. Most of the time, when Jesus goes on a journey in the Gospels, there is a physical healing that takes place, the call of an apostle or disciple, a miracle by which Jesus multiplies food so that thousands can now eat, or even a confrontation with the Pharisees. Yet, on this particular day, Jesus is on a journey and we are not at first sure of its purpose. In fact, before we learn anything else about his trip, we learn he was tired. This was the journey we read in the Gospel of St. John. The Gospel tells us, "He had to pass through Samaria...Jesus, tired from his journey, sat down there at the well. It was about noon" (John 4:4, 6b). There is a lot in those two sentences. Jesus is traveling from Judea to Galilee (John 4:3). The Gospel does not say he *decided* to pass through Samaria. It does not say he thought it would be nice to pass through Samaria. It simply says he *had* to pass through Samaria. He *had* to. When the Gospel tells us that Jesus *had* to pass through Samaria, the Greek word it uses for *had* is *edei*. *Edei* is no ordinary word. This word means *it was necessary* that Jesus pass through Samaria to accomplish his journey. But if we look at a map, we quickly learn that Jesus could have traveled from Judea to Galilee by any of several routes. Therefore, it was certainly not *geographically* necessary that Jesus pass through Samaria on this particular day.

In addition, we learn something else about this journey of Jesus. The evangelist notes Jesus is *tired* from his journey. He has evidently traveled a long way. In fact, Jesus is so tired he *sits down*. He sits down at a well. By sitting down, Jesus does something else. He takes the position of the teacher. Sitting down, in the time of the Bible, was no ordinary gesture. The teacher taught from the seated position. When Jesus sits down, he is showing himself to be the teacher. Recall that he will also do this at the beginning of the Sermon on the Mount: The Gospel tells us he went up the mountain and sat down (Matt 5:1). Even though he is tired, he is never too tired to reach out to us to teach us the way to the Kingdom. In fact, his tiredness is a sign of a profoundly deeper reality. Jesus is the Son of God. His entire mission is one in which he pours himself out for us and for our salvation.

When Jesus sits down in Samaria, he does not sit down just anywhere or at a random place. He sits down at a well. In any time or place, the well is quickly recognized as a special place. It is a location of refreshment and a source of renewed strength. Yet, in the biblical world, the well has a deeper significance still. In the Old Testament, the well is a place of a unique encounter: the betrothal. The well is the place where future spouses meet, where future marriages are arranged. It is the meeting place of spousal love.[1] Isaac and Rebekah, Jacob and Rachel, and Moses and Zipporah are all betrothed after meeting—or after being seen—at a well (Gen 24; Gen 29; Exod 2). Jesus, on his journey, necessarily passes by the place of chaste spousal love on his journey and he sits down there as the teacher. Thus, the well, on a deeper level, is a place of communion.

Jesus stops at the well at no ordinary time. The text of St. John recounts, "It was about noon" (John 4:6b). The record of the time appears at first merely to set the scene. But a deeper meaning again is at work: At noon, the sun is directly overhead and its heat is intense. People withdraw. It is the lonely time. It is at this hour on Good Friday that Jesus will go to the cross—for the salvation of the woman of Samaria and for us (John 19:14).

SHE HAD SUFFERED MUCH

The Gospel text continues: "A woman of Samaria came to draw water" (John 4:7). Time and again in St. John's Gospel, we find that Jesus is one-on-one with a person. It was necessary that Jesus pass through Samaria, not for geographic reasons, but for this woman and her salvation. As we will find out later in the account, she has suffered much at the hands of many men. Jesus will address this later in the parable: "You have had five husbands, and the one you have now is not your husband." Numbers stand for more than a mathematical count in the Bible; numbers have much more to tell us. For instance, the number five does not just mean this woman had five husbands. The number five also stands for the five senses. St. Bonaventure mentions this very meaning and draws our attention to a connection between the number five in the account of the rich man in the Gospel of St. Luke (Luke 16:28), who asks Abraham to send the poor man Lazarus to his five brothers: "By the number five is understood that they had been given over to the five senses of the body," according to what is said to the Samaritan woman (John 4:18): 'You have had five husbands....'"[2] The rich man was indulgent in the pleasures of the five senses. In the five husbands of the Samaritan woman, we can discern a reference to the trap of the indulgence of the five senses, an indulgence which prevents her from meeting the Lord. Until now.

Her history may indicate the reason she approaches the well at this unusual time. Having had five husbands, she most likely has a reputation in the town. This reputation has made her somewhat of an outcast, and an object of scorn. Ordinarily, people come to the well in the early morning or later evening when the temperature is cooler. Yet, she comes at noon, when the heat is unforgiving. Her embarrassment has sidelined her to this desolate and difficult time for her task of raising water. If she came with the crowd in the cool of the morning or early evening, the glances, pointing, and murmuring would be simply too much to endure. She would rather endure the scorching heat than the painful glares of her neighbors.

The timing is perfect. It is at noon when he will mount his cross and cry out in his loneliness and thirst. He is here for her in her loneliness. He thirsts here at this noon hour, as he will on the cross at the noon hour. He asks for a drink (John 4:7b). He longs to fulfill the mission of salvation.

Jesus meets the Samaritan woman in the midst of her daily tasks. He has come on a long journey. She is in her familiar painful place. Jesus, the Good Shepherd who seeks the lost sheep, follows us to rescue us from our painful places as well. Many faithful Christians, and many well-meaning people of good will, like Tom and Nancy, find themselves isolated in the lonely, scorching heat of the effects of Internet pornography and cybersex. Even in this contemporary moment of pain, Jesus sits down as the teacher. He comes to what is to be the place of love that Tom, and perhaps we, ourselves, have turned into a place of indulgence. He comes to us in the time of our intensity and embarrassment. He wants to save us, to begin a new narrative in our life and to heal us.

CHAPTER 3

"EVERYONE WHO DRINKS THIS WATER WILL BE THIRSTY AGAIN" (JOHN 4:13)

THE CAUSES OF INTERNET PORNOGRAPHY USE

Before Tom got caught, he had actually functioned quite well on the surface. When he was younger, he got fairly good grades in school. He was employee of the month several times. He now makes a good salary. He is a smooth and effective manager, but he has been tortured inside...for years.

His toxic and troublesome patterns did not arise simply out of nowhere. They arose from his pain, and this comes from the hurts of life...his wounds. Tom, like us, does not like to show his wounds, and in fact, pretends he has no wounds. He covers them up with the latest fashions. He seeks to drown the pain with passing pleasures. He convinces himself that making the next deal, reaching the next payday, finding the next sale, earning the next bonus, experiencing the numbness of the next happy hour, entering the next relationship, or winning the next argument will prove that he is worthwhile. He has long attempted to cover his wounds with his performance and results, but success has proven a weak and ineffective antidote to his personal, internal pain. He has tried for years to cover his pain with substances and activities. Cybersex is a sensation-based activity. The pain that drives Tom's use of Internet pornography emerges from his long-standing wounds.

WOUNDS AND WALLS

What causes Tom's wounds? His wounds come from an early experience of pain. Tom looks put together on the outside. He arrives on time, double checks his reports, and is well mannered. Yet, Tom has grown up in a culture in which the dominant mindset disregards the dignity of human life, the beauty of marriage and family, and the sacredness of human sexuality. Sooner or later, the sins of the culture, these overriding societal trends, trickle down and cause pain in very personal ways. The fast-paced, all-or-nothing chaos of the secularist ways of popular society often leave scars: These scars come from the sins associated with rejection of the dignity of human life, traumatic conflict, and family division. Tom's wounds came from when someone very important to him may have hurt him. They may have done this directly or inadvertently. They probably thought they were helping, not hurting Tom. But the painful ways of a culture that rejects the dignity of human life and the beauty of human love will sooner or later creep disguised into what should be the most noble of places. It may have been a teacher, parent, coach, or friend. Perhaps they yelled or screamed at Tom because he didn't quite measure up. They thought it would motivate him, but instead, they pressured and hurt him. Even worse, perhaps they emotionally neglected him, or physically struck him. They may have continually and unduly pressured Tom, threatened him, or blamed him. They may have been chronically forgetful of his legitimate needs, casually rejected Tom, or had been aggressively severe toward his attempts at genuine independence. They may have been too strict or too permissive, or they may have dismissed him or used him to meet their own unmet needs. Tom probably had to walk on eggshells until he inevitably stepped on a landmine.

Tom's wounds are like our own. Very often, we were simply trying to express a feeling: We were tired, lonely, upset, afraid, angry, curious, sad, or happy. When we expressed some of these feelings, we met a wall. The prevailing culture tells us to show no weakness or vulnerability. In fact, the vulnerable are at high risk in the modern culture. Someone told us, perhaps on a regular basis, that a B in spelling was just not good enough. Perhaps spilling the milk at dinner triggered a parent's bottled-up rage. Maybe our parents chose to work extra hours rather than come to our game, even though they promised to be there this time. Perhaps we were left to our own devices in the midst of hectic schedules and parental break-ups. We may have felt distraught that we seemed to be off everyone's list: We were not athletic enough to be on the team, intelligent enough to be in honors class, or popular enough to be invited to the right parties. Perhaps our parents gave more attention to their arguments with one another and their competition with business rivals than to their own children. People who were important to us may have reacted strongly and negatively to our natural and honest feelings of vulnerability. We had to choose between our feelings and our parents. Over time, we were conditioned to respond in painful ways. We chose to hide our feelings and stuff them away. We may have a messy internal world of feelings and reactions that caused us pain at one time or another. We felt that our feelings were improper and wrong, and now we cringe when this hidden world nears the surface. Our painful feelings often accompany things we have spent so long trying to fix. We pretend the hurt and pain do not exist, but for things that do not exist, they certainly take up a lot of our time and consume a considerable amount of our personal energy.

Our parents may have loved us too little or too much. We may have felt neglected and had to perform more for attention.

Our caregivers and early role models may have shown rejection, abandonment, or chronic dysfunction. Or, our caregivers did the best they could, but were unable to shield us from early loss associated with divorce or death. There may have been arguing and fighting at home, name calling, and bullying at school. Some individuals were teased about their weight or put down for their appearance. It is easy to label people and to be labeled by people. We often live down to our labels, and labels can easily pave the way to trouble, intimacy deficits, and even to pathologies.

Coupled with missed opportunities, quick judgments, strong sibling competition in a home with scarce rewards and harsh consequences, a deficit developed deep in our hearts. Some people's memories of home life are callous rather than warm. These hurts tragically expand if there was also emotional, physical, or sexual abuse, and other forms of neglect and mistreatment.

Experiences of pain lead Tom, and perhaps us, to seek comfort in more immediate forms of pleasure and compensation. Children who encountered these painful conditions often internalized the trauma and compounded it by blaming themselves for the situation. Perhaps Tom added to the pain and confusion by blaming himself, and for a long time, believed the hurtful words and actions were somehow his own fault. Under such circumstances, Tom's heart was bruised. The bruise is deepened and compounded by the fact that it was someone important to Tom who inflicted it. As young victims, they attempted to do the best they could with what they had available to them. They may have ignored their painful patterns of indulgence for years, believing the distress and unpredictability was how everyone else in the world lived too…that it was normal.

The denial may have begun early, and gave way to long-standing, unresolved, and unhealthy patterns of avoidance. Today, the clouds may remain, and the shadows may stretch out for some distance. Now a grown-up, Tom may be angry and depressed on the inside. Although he goes through the motions of adulthood, it is difficult for him to find his confidence. Internet pornography appears to be the quick fix, the soothing solution and the anesthesia that dulls the pain. Yet, in truth, it only compounds the original wound. It does not help that the culture repeatedly tells Tom that the most pleasure for the most people is the purpose and goal of life.

Tom might not be very aware of the wounds, but nonetheless, his past actions and missed opportunities haunt Tom and many people daily. The old battlefields and sins leave deeply entrenched thought and belief patterns that still influence his daily life. He might feel resentful, regretful, or resistant and not know why. When he was hurt early in life, he put up walls. Walls come in all shapes and sizes: walls of anger, control, intensity, activity, and humor; walls of annoyance, irritation, depression, and ego. Tom spent a great deal of energy attempting to justify and legitimize his walls. The seeming impenetrability of his walls prevents him from turning to forgiveness and mercy and instead diverts him to searching out sinful coping mechanisms, self-centered excuses, and immoral escapes to deal with the distance introduced by pretending. Simply put, wounds arose when, at one point in Tom's history, love was turned into fear. The greatest and rarest of all alchemy is to transform fear back into love, to turn from sin to forgiveness.

THE NATURE OF PORNOGRAPHY

The *Catechism of the Catholic Church* teaches that:

Pornography consists in removing real or simulated sexual acts from the intimacy of the partners, in order to display them deliberately to third parties. It offends against chastity because it perverts the conjugal act, the intimate giving of spouses to each other. It does grave injury to the dignity of its participants (actors, vendors, the public), since each one becomes an object of base pleasure and illicit profit for others. It immerses all who are involved in the illusion of a fantasy world. It is a grave offense. Civil authorities should prevent the production and distribution of pornographic materials.[1]

The *Catechism* highlights that pornography is an offense against both human dignity and chastity. The teaching of the *Catechism* is founded on the human person created in the image and likeness of God (Gen 1:26–27), the call to chastity as expressed in the sixth commandment, "You shall not commit adultery" (Exod 20:14; Deut 5:18), and the fulfillment of this commandment in the teaching of Jesus in the Beatitudes, in particular, the sixth beatitude, "Blessed are the clean of heart" (Matt 5:8). In the Sermon on the Mount, Jesus locates the heart as the center of morality: "You have heard that it was said, 'You shall not commit adultery.' But I say to you, everyone who looks at a woman with lust has already committed adultery with her in his heart" (Matt 5:27-28). The Church teaches that we reach such purity, the successful integration of the sexual appetite, through the virtue of temperance. The virtues in general, and temperance in particular, are not unreachable spiritualized ideals meant for the very few. The virtues arise in our lives from the action of the Holy Spirit. The Holy Spirit is always seeking inroads such that we can be drawn deep inside the mystery of Jesus and realize that we live the Christian life not on the basis of our own strength, but that all things are transformed by Christ who conquers all. Sanctity and holiness are not old-fashioned; they are a daily way of life.

Man is called to blessed happiness. Because of sin, the adventure to happiness is filled with traps. False illusions of happiness spring up before us. These promise happiness through self-ishness. Healing means restoring the ability to discern and discover true and authentic happiness and the ability to distinguish the telltale signs of false promises of happiness that only appear alluring, but are very dangerous. So often today we find a mistaken notion of the meaning of happiness. We doubt that happiness is possible until all of our intangible needs are met. We lock ourselves into a perfect idea of personal happiness in which all of our needs are satisfied as soon as possible: We think that this is the only way to be happy. Authentic and genuine happiness is not lost in an unreachable past or locked in an impossible future. It is close to us if only we begin to treasure the present moment, forgive, and begin to follow the path of virtue.[2] This is the proper way to integrate the sexual urge in response to the call to holiness.

All offenses against human dignity and chastity are a result of the effects of original sin and personal sin (Rom 5:12; Gen 3). Because human nature is wounded and weakened due to sin, we fall for the traps: We know it is good to pray, to eat well, to exercise, and to study, but there are times when we attempt to cut corners and take the easy way. We vow to begin a healthy diet at night, but the next morning, we stop at the convenience store and select the frosted donut with the multicolored sprinkles. We know it is true that study is appropriate for school, and that rest is important for the next day of work, yet we stay up late and don't crack the books. Regarding human sexuality, the trap of promiscuity leads us to seek to treat ourselves and others as objects to be used for pleasure. Promiscuity promises happiness through physical pleasure, but the self-centeredness inherent in such actions always harms the nuptial and spousal meaning of the body.[3] In particular, as regards human sexuality, the temptation is to reduce, possess, and control the other: "Your urge shall be for your husband and he shall rule over you" (Gen 3:16). In his fallen state, man experiences the uproar and disorder of the appetites, which often and frequently war against that which is true and good. This is true in a particular way of the sensual appetite, and the pursuit of pleasures of the body. Pornography is the hallmark of promiscuity in modern culture. The production and use of pornography is a grave sin. The United States Conference of Catholic Bishops has taught that "producing, marketing, or indulging in pornography" constitute "actions which involve grave matter" and "are serious violations of the law of love of God and of neighbor."[4] The Pontifical Council for Social Communications noted in "Pornography and Violence in the Communications Media: A Pastoral Response" in 1989 that, "In the worst cases, pornography can act as an inciting or reinforcing agent, a kind of accomplice, in the behavior of dangerous sex offenders—child molesters, rapists and killers."[5]

Already in the mid-twentieth century, Karol Wojtyla, who became Pope John Paul II in October 1978, noted that pornography was a very broad problem in which the sexual element was accentuated at the expense of the complete personal element of human sexuality. Wojtyla pointed out that human happiness was fragmented by pornography, which already at that time had become a deliberate trend.[6]

SOME DIFFERENCES BETWEEN CONVENTIONAL PORNOGRAPHY AND INTERNET PORNOGRAPHY

The answer for Tom is found only in the grace of Jesus Christ experienced in and through the Church. We will examine this foundational and important reality later in this book. One of the early steps in Tom's journey of healing is discernment and the truth about the sin he has been committing and the elements of its occasion. Such self-knowledge is very important in the growth of humility. As Tom begins to grow in virtue, he can benefit from learning about the true nature of the trap he was so often caught in. This can assist him in avoiding it in the future. Pornography comes in at least two general forms: conventional and Internet. Conventional pornography consists of photography, film, drawings, pictures, narrative, or story as found in magazines, books, and videos. A magazine always has a last page. A video always has a last frame. Such individual formats are limited. Internet pornography consists of downloading, retrieving, sending, trading, buying, selling, receiving, or storing sexually explicit photographs, film, conduct, videos, streaming videos, subscriptions to porn sites and archives, instant messages, as well as entering sexually explicit chat rooms, arranging to meet persons online for sexual acts, masturbating while online, and trading sexually explicit pictures and text through cellular phones, an activity known as "sexting." Such activities are often preceded by explicit electronic flirtatious behaviors including types of role-playing and creating a fictitious online personality. Four million pornographic Web sites have virtually no last page, but are linked together in a seemingly inexhaustible supply of pornographic content. Pornography, once thought by society to be a problem, is now an industry and a lifestyle.

The difference between conventional and Internet pornography becomes more clear when Tom learns about the four general groups as they relate to the phenomenon of conventional pornography. The first group consists of those people who, as they grew up, were aware at some point of the phenomenon of pornography, but have never experienced any substantial use of pornography. For this group, sufficient personal boundaries were in place such that no attachment to pornography developed. They remain removed and distanced from any fixation or attraction to the use of pornography. For example, although they were aware of pornography, and perhaps even curious about it, they did not take the risks associated with buying or keeping pornography. Their own personal boundaries and life experiences were such that they would never even think about going to an adult bookstore or phoning the number of an adult sex line.

A second group consists of persons such as Tom, who became aware of pornography and experimented with the viewing and use of pornography earlier in life. Circumstance, curiosity, and poor personal boundaries intersected and yielded to further exploration of pornography. Such persons may have seen pornography passed around a locker room, heard it referenced in sexually explicit jokes, received pornographic e-mails or ads on the computer, pursued curiosity brought about by R-rated movies, found it in the family home, or experienced some measure of peer pressure to buy it or look at it. Such factors set the context for experimentation through viewing pornographic magazines and videos. Factors such as a negative social network, early sexual trauma, or lack of a nurturing home life may intensify and augment circumstances that present risk for exploration of pornography. At the same time, as the person's growth and maturity advanced, they realized the mistakes and indulgences of immaturity were improper. At times, they may periodically regress to indulgent patterns, which they recognize as morally wrong. They make recourse to the life of grace in the sacraments and seek the strength to return to the life of virtue. Pornography is not a fixation for such persons, but its nature and use is not foreign either.

A third group consists of those who, having become aware of pornography, have developed a pattern of regular and frequent use. They may experience a binge pattern in which they stop for a time and then use pornography a great deal. Science tells us that such use can open and activate neural pathways in the brain that habituate the behavior.[7] Recurrent use may be punctuated with extended periods of nonuse but are often followed by intense periods of frequent use. They experience pornography as enticing and have established a pattern of use that is somewhat common and recurrent.

A fourth group are the compulsive users of pornography. The habitual experience of use of pornography at this level is almost daily. They are willing to go to great lengths to obtain pornographic materials and maintain such in a collection. A significant amount of their time is devoted to pornography. Although binging is possible here, the use is very regular and involvement heavy.

The boundaries between the four categories of persons are marked by the fact that those in the earlier categories are strengthened by virtue at least to the point that they are not willing to take risks to obtain conventional pornography. If one were to buy a magazine or rent an adult video, the clerk may recognize them, the materials may be found, and the risk is enough to deter any habitual use. The person avoids the risks not merely out of fear of punishment, but out of a real desire not to lead others to sin and to follow that which is morally beautiful and good.

Attendant with the shift from conventional pornography to Internet pornography, each group has faced the pressure to move to the next level of vulnerability: Those who before would hardly even think of using conventional pornography, are more curious about Internet pornography; those who were curious about conventional pornography are now, with the availability of Internet pornography, thinking about it more often; those who were in the intermittent binge pattern with conventional pornography are now, with Internet pornography, prone to be more compulsive; those who were compulsive with conventional pornography are now, with Internet pornography, likely to be in an avalanche. The classification of user is often a continuum: from the curious to the casual, to the chronic to the compulsive.[8] When the Digital Revolution crisscrossed the fault lines of the Sexual Revolution, many people were led right to a dead end...or in many instances, a treacherous cliff. And many marched right over and plunged deep into pain.

FACTORS INFLUENCING PORNOGRAPHY USE

Three factors, in particular, account for the susceptibility of persons to Internet pornography: increased accessibility, financial affordability, and perceived anonymity.[9] Tom knows that the Internet is accessible twenty-four hours a day, seven days a week. Before the Internet, Tom could avoid pornography by simply not visiting the magazine rack of the local store. Now, he knows that the images are a click away in the family room or bedroom on the computer. He is very vulnerable. He would never have taken the risk of purchasing or keeping conventional pornography, but now Tom believes there is little or no risk of discovery with the use of the Internet. He mistakenly believes that when he logs off or deletes the history of Web sites he visited, the evidence goes away and the trail vanishes. He finds in the computer screen a filter that he thinks prevents discovery of his identity and protects his privacy. This is commonly known as dissociative anonymity.[10] Tom has the sensation that he is eavesdropping or wearing a cloak of invisibility as he visits pornographic Web sites and converses online. He thinks no one knows it is him, but, in reality, once he logs on he can be easily tracked. He even creates fictional identities through which to interact. He fails to understand that forensic computer analysts can access deleted histories and cleaned computer drives. Before the Internet, Tom did not use pornography. Because he was never willing to pay the price of securing various issues of magazines or videos, he developed a positive and strong disposition to chastity. But now the availability and perceived anonymity tempt him repeatedly. He doesn't think twice about using his computer at work to view pornography, which, in addition to the moral issues already discussed, introduces complex legal issues.

THE CYCLIC NATURE OF INTERNET PORNOGRAPHY USE

Tom's self-knowledge can also benefit from learning there are specific behavior patterns with pornography use that often manifest a cyclic nature:[11] Tom experiences the agitation of the sexual appetite. Boredom leads to curiosity. Curiosity leads to experimentation. Experimentation quickly escalates to habit and the search for a new high. This stimulation can emerge from his memories of previously viewed pornographic images or from a semierotic scene in a movie or television show. Gratification of the sexual drive through fantasy, conversation, masturbation, or sense indulgence coalesces to further stimulate the sexual appetite. Gratification leads, ironically, not to fulfillment, but to emptiness, despair, irritability, and further personal difficulties. Gratification routinely interferes with integration and healing.

In Tom's case, the cycle of use begins with Tom being preoccupied with finding a time to log onto the Internet.[12] He finds it difficult to concentrate on other tasks and is distracted by the interruptive and ongoing occasion of sin; particularly of thoughts and daydreams about past images viewed and finding a situation of privacy with access to a computer. Tom's mood grows more agitated and disturbed by interruptions that impede his access to privacy and the Internet. The persistence of this preoccupation may easily wear away his resistance if he does not make recourse to grace-filled interventions and prayer.

The second phase of the cycle initiates when Tom capitulates and begins to seek out access to the Internet, and is willing to take risks to do so. If the typical routine for logging on is available, he carries it out: He makes excuses to be alone. He closes the door, draws the shades, turns on the computer. The screen glows, and he logs on.

At each passing step, Tom is engaging the ritual cues, the series of seemingly incidental details such as closing the door and turning on the screen, which are associated more and more directly with the anticipated comfort of the perceived payoff. These cues and patterns are carried out unconsciously. They signal the anticipated arrival of the pornographic images—the way the sound of the ice in the tumbler signals the entrancement of alcohol for the alcoholic. Such cues also have an extensive effect deep in Tom's brain and psyche: Natural painkillers and endorphins are released into the circulatory and nervous system, and bring rapid relief and exhilaration with each step.

The third step of the cycle arrives as Tom then acts out. He views the images, surfs the net for more images, enters sexually explicit chat rooms, and links to any number of sites. This is the time of the high. After a period of viewing that can last hours, the process often culminates in masturbation.

The fourth phase of the cycle initiates as the pace of the excitement deteriorates, the thrill quickly wears off, and Tom emerges from the viewing often with feelings of guilt and shame. These feelings mutate quickly into despair. Tom may attempt strong resolutions never to access pornography again, and perhaps even to swear off technology altogether. He may cancel the contract with his online service provider and even throw away his computer. In this phase, negative beliefs about the self become further entrenched. While the entire cycle is fraught with loneliness and isolation, this fourth phase is especially potent. The cycle comes full circle when, after having mulled over the despair and been saturated with shame and self-accusation, Tom seeks relief through preoccupation with pornography, as the first stage of the cycle comes around again and the process is repeated.

WARNING SIGNS

If Tom were paying attention, he would have seen several warning signs that indicate problematic online behavior. The warning signs include lying about one's online activity and significant amounts of time spent on the Internet to the extent that time online is interfering with regular life and routine obligations. Tom may have a blank affect, lack of emotional regulation, simmering resentment, lack of basic friendship skills, and entitlement tendencies. Other warning signs are secrecy about online activities, concealing one's identity while online, maintaining a collection of favorite pornographic Web sites, masturbating while online, deleting the history of visited Web sites, separate online access, or the use of separate computers. An advanced warning sign of at-risk online behavior is arranging to meet with strangers found online.

EFFECTS

The effects of pornography use are manifold and the victims numerous. It is in no way a victimless activity. The first and most significant effect of unchaste behavior, online or otherwise, is participation in grave sin. If Tom carried out these actions with full consent of the will and sufficient reflection, such actions are mortally sinful. The first and primary remedy for such sinful acts always remains the grace and mercy of God in the sacrament of penance.

Other effects flow from this grave situation and behavior. As pornography intrudes on the culture, we witness the erosion of married love, the undermining of the family, heightening of risks to children, an upgrade in promiscuity and infidelity, earlier onset of sexual behavior, and the increased risk of sexually transmitted diseases, personal instability because of compulsive sexual behavior, as well as financial and legal impropriety.[13]

Tom also learns pornography erodes respect for women.[14] Pornography use leads men to search for the anonymous, one-dimensional image that perfectly corresponds to their fantasy. Imagination is blunted in day-to-day life, as fantasy becomes a substitute for real events, authentic relationships, and substantial communication. The claim that pornography is a victimless crime is inaccurate in both the immediate and long-term analysis. Many participants and actors in pornographic depictions are pressured into such activities to earn money to support drug addiction. The use of pornography thus supports the painful behavior of persons in dire situations. The long-term effects of use of pornography include the breakdown of marriage, crisis in family life, divorce, and loss of employment.[15]

THE MYTH OF GRATIFICATION

On the surface, the use of pornography purports to bring relief of sexual tension. On a deeper level, the gratification associated with pornography distracts the user as it momentarily numbs the pain of our chronic wounds. Men employ the mesmerizing thrill of the sexual high to counter everything from boredom to pain. Human sexuality is a life-giving and love-giving reality. This is why it is properly expressed only in the permanent, faithful, and fruitful bond of marriage between one man and one woman—because life and love are so important and meaningful, they take place only within this permanent bond. Marriage is ordered to the procreation and education of children and the faithful expression of the unitive good of man and woman in the communion of persons.[16] Human sexuality is the matrix along which the gift of self is bestowed and received in marriage. Through sin and temptation we are led to take advantage of our life-giving and love-giving gifts, and to use them for ourselves rather than for life and love. We are tempted to use them not for life and love, but only for pleasure…and in using them for pleasure to use them *against* life and love. Men are conditioned through pornography to reduce love to sex, and sex to stimulation and gratification. They get used to their bodies and drives and those of others to being only about self-centered comfort through a short-term payoff. In this, they strip the gears of love so love is not about a gift of self for life and love, but is actually reversed, inversed, to be about self-gratification. The thrill of stimulation associated with sexual energy and the power it carries actually blinds men so that all they see is the immediate gratification, not the doubling down of the pain in the destructive short-term and long-term sinful consequences. Men think what they are doing with pornography is about sex, but it is really about gratification, and this gratification is not at the service of life and love because pornography is always about using ourselves and the other person. Love does not use, ever. Love gives. Often, the gratification and use are employed as a means to block a deeper pain that men are not even fully conscious of, about which they are in denial. Deep down, they gratify themselves not because they want to feel love, but because *they do not want to feel pain*. People bury the pain of past hurts in shallow graves in our memory. People feel that pain in daily distress, emotional immaturity, anxiety, agitation, and frustration. Emotional pain drives many problematic behaviors. This is not a condemnation, but a fact. They then seek to quell the pain through turning to things that feel good such as food, drink, and sex. The tragic irony is that the very pain that men seek to heal through the use of pornography only grows deeper with its use.

CHAPTER 4

"FOR YOU HAVE HAD FIVE HUSBANDS" (JOHN 4:18)

HITTING BOTTOM

Jesus speaks the word of truth to the Samaritan woman. He provides an invitation and then gently and clearly identifies the difficulties and sins of her past. Once the truth is spoken and made known, the inner work of healing can begin. In the story at the beginning of Chapter 1, Tom's wife discovered his online behavior after Tom fell asleep at the screen with the images easily accessible and visible. The information technology (IT) supervisor at Tom's place of employment could have also discovered his online activity and confronted Tom through the human resources department. His son or daughter may have discovered Tom's Internet history on the computer.

In fact, "Tom" actually could fit any of the various scenarios below[1]:

- Tom is a happily married man. He has always been responsible, paid his bills on time, is effective at work, and raised four children. His wife is out with friends and the kids are at sleepovers on a Saturday night. He glances at the clock and realizes he has binged online for six or seven hours, cruising from one porn site to the next. He scares himself. He senses a disconnect.

- Tom is the trustworthy, recently engaged young man who is eager to be conscientious and sensible in his preparation for marriage and volunteers regularly at church. Yet, he feels powerless before the force of the urge to seek out pornographic images online. Tom even keeps a mental list of his favorite porn sites. After the first hour of loneliness, he logs on and visits each. As he goes to church on Sunday morning, he feels like a hypocrite.

- Tom is the college student who sees his grades plummet and his scholarship fade because he links from one site to the next on the library computer instead of preparing for final examinations.

- Tom is a businessman who travels frequently for work. He believes he must always be the top seller, the leader of sales, and spends every waking hour strategizing and scheming for new methods and higher returns. He believes he must continually prove his worth. He checks and rechecks the charts, market analysis, income forecasts, and performance records. The tension of travel, the stress of managing his portfolio of accounts, and the loneliness of being away from his wife and children wear down his resistance and he seeks relief in routinely accessing Internet pornography in hotel rooms. Tom's wife opens the mail one day and sees transactions for pay pornography sites. She tearfully confronts him.

- Tom is an office worker who is in the habit of accessing porn on a work computer. His screen is partially visible from the office door. He keeps a wary eye if anyone should approach. He sees, out of the corner of his eye, a female colleague coming near to ask for his assistance. He moves the cursor to click quickly out of the screen.

The computer freezes. The screen remains. She is almost within view of the screen. Tom jumps up and cuts off her approach and takes her question. He was almost caught. The IT supervisor at work posts a new policy regarding Internet use and not accessing pornographic sites. Tom wonders, "Is he talking about me?"

• Tom is a young man, technologically savvy but very emotionally vulnerable and socially inept, who initiates contact with a woman in an online chat room. He is shocked when she sends an e-mail message asking to meet.

Perhaps Tom is Father Tom: One day he is in a liturgy committee meeting at his parish assignment. When he isn't drumming his fingers on the conference room table he is doodling. He has scribbled all over the March liturgy committee agenda as if it is another Picasso. The others at the meeting have noticed Father Tom shifting in his seat for the last half hour. What they don't know is that his thoughts are about anything but Picasso: "I can't wait to get online. When will this meeting be over? When will he stop talking so we can just all leave? How many times can you plan the Easter Vigil anyway? Not that we're planning, because it's everything that he wants to do. Why am I here? I can't wait to get online." His thoughts, concentration, and ruminations are directed to that all-important time when he closes his office door. At the end of the meeting, he departs briskly as if there were a fire drill. Committee members wonder if they made him mad somehow…again. He disappears down the hallway to his office and closes the door. As the knob clicks, he relaxes a little. Alone at last. He moves from preoccupation to ritual, the second phase of the addictive cycle. The sound of the door closing is a cue. He is getting closer to his pay-off. "I'll only stay on fifteen minutes. Last time was seven hours. Only fifteen minutes this time. That'll be an improvement." Using his personal laptop, he logs on through the

Internet service provider via a phone line so the IT person on staff won't be able to monitor where he goes online. The whistle sound of the search modem relaxes him. The second cue. Painkillers are released in his blood stream as each cue passes. The wait is worth it. The homepage appears. He relaxes more. He moves to the behavior stage of the addictive cycle. Unlike the meeting, he can control everything in this room, or so he thinks. He drums his fingers across the keys. Anything but Picasso emerges. The office door opens five hours later. He leaves feeling guilty and despondent. His personal life and pastoral ministry are spiraling out of control. He did it all again. Although he thinks and believes he is alone, there are more and more church leaders, feeling overwhelmed, who struggle with the same difficulty.

What do all of these situations have in common? They all involve persons who are waiting to hit rock bottom, where, despite its pain, a moment of realization of truth can arise. The inner feelings of despondency…sensing a pervasive disconnect…feeling like a hypocrite…the awareness that one is keeping secrets…painful confrontation and intervention…almost getting caught. All of these persons are waiting for a moment of realization of the truth. The moment of realization can come in a variety of ways, and it is always a sobering moment. The person who sexualizes their online activities ordinarily experiences some degree of guilt. Guilt is not always bad; in fact, it can be considerably healthy, such as when a person senses that their online actions do not correspond with who they are the rest of the time. Good guilt is a first, all-important step in the right direction: It is God calling us home; it is the real us hearing his call. Guilt often stands in sharp contrast to our own rigidly perfectionist ideals. The crisis of hitting rock bottom is the opportunity to pivot to a life of authenticity and virtue.

The one who has turned to Internet pornography might believe they are simply very weak and predetermined to give in to acting out. They might wonder if resistance is even worthwhile. They might blame themselves and feel they are fated to lose this struggle. It is then they must consider all that has happened to them. Whatever the burdens of life have been for them, somehow they got through. If their early life was difficult, if patterns go a long way back, if they believe they have had all the bad breaks, they cannot deny that nonetheless something is living inside of them that must be appreciated. Somehow they got through it all. Even though wounded and perhaps down-and-out, they are alive. They were strong enough to make it through and they survived. They were strong enough to pick up this book. They are not beaten. A large part of the healing includes Tom hitting rock bottom and using that as a new opportunity to begin to heal.

Hitting bottom is similar to the experience of the Prodigal Son. After the son had gone through the portion of the father's estate that was his, the Gospel tells us that he began to be in need. He attached himself to one of the propertied class, and began to feed the animals and longed to eat their food. Notice the connection between neediness and attachment. Fueled by his neediness, he indulged his hunger and appetites until they got the best of him. He wasted his inheritance; he thought he had destroyed the relationships that should have been most important to him. Then one day, in his need, "Coming to his senses, he thought…" (Luke 15:17). This was his moment of hitting bottom. He was confronted with and realized the truth of his circumstances. He was alone—broken and broke—and had nowhere to turn. He had hit rock bottom.

Notice, however, what it is that turns him to his senses. It is the *look of the Father*. The Father, since the Son has left, has been *gazing into the distance*. The English translation says that "his father caught sight of him…" (Luke 15:20). This translation does not completely capture the sense of the original Greek text. The text implies the father was gazing *into* the distant land…

and, at the same time, the father was gazing *into the distance between himself and his son*.[2] One could say the father was gazing at his son while the son *was a long way off*. When we hit rock bottom, a lot more is going on than just learning the true nature of our painful circumstances. From the moment we go off track, God the Father *gazes into the distance* between us and him. It is his look, his grace, even when we are in sin, that wakes us up again and inspires in us (literally, breathes into us) the desire and longing for repentance. This is known as *prevenient grace*, a grace that comes to us to encourage us to turn back to God. The Tradition calls this the sorrow of heart (*compuntio cordis*) that prompts us to turn again to the mercy of God.

A similar moment of realization comes for the Samaritan woman when Jesus says to her: "You are right in saying, 'I do not have a husband.' For you have had five husbands, and the one you have now is not your husband. What you have said is true" (John 4:17–18). This is the truth she knew all along, but never wanted to hear. This is why she avoided everyone and came to the well at midday. This moment of realization is hard, but it brings a clarity that is crucial. Jesus indicates the woman has spoken the truth. She has emerged from denial to glimpse and gauge the true nature of her circumstances, situation, and actions. When the charade is over, the healing can start.

This is the case with Tom. The rush that was so entertaining a moment ago, that Tom wished would never end, flees and leaves him stranded. Hitting bottom, being caught by his wife, is the moment of realization when Tom finally glimpses reality. Up to this moment, he has been absorbed with fantasy. Ironically, the moment of hitting bottom is the only real moment in the experience of the user of pornography. It can be, finally, after so much illusion and deception, a moment of hope and a decisive turning point.

The moment of hope can be defused, however. Initially, the shock jolts the user into awareness as to what he is actually in how subjects were presented. In cop shows, for example, the businessman was almost always the villain. The military came in for severe hits. Religious people were usually hypocrites and charlatans. Small towns were dangerous, smoldering pits of evil, especially racist evil. On comedies, fun was made of conservatives and anyone with money was a fool.

I observed this for a few years at UCSC and afterward, on my faithful, flickering Panasonic. Then I wrote a book, called *The View from Sunset Boulevard.* The book had not just the observations I had made of TV shows' sociological points of view, but also the view of many TV writers and producers on the same subjects: business, capitalism, faith, small towns, the military. Through interviews, I found that the views of the people who make the TV shows were almost identical; in fact, they were identical to the views shown on the TV shows. What we saw when we watched TV was not an approximation of reality or a consensus view of American life. No, it was the projection of what the top producers and writers in Hollywood believed to be the way life was.

The book got a fantastic amount of notice. It was damned by liberals and people in Hollywood — with some notable exceptions — and loved by conservatives. It was used as a text in universities for years. Now, many years have passed and hardly anyone remembers the book.

> at many times of the day — pornography of sex and pornography of violence.

everywhere. Some are about dangerous or unpleasant work. Why? Where does that come from?

On the scripted shows, there are now far more than the three network shows. There is a breathtaking amount of news, especially financial news. This is, well, new, and has gripped the nation by the throat, pouring "news" (largely fake) down people's throats, whether they have any idea of its truth or not. Dancing and talent shows are huge, although possibly dwindling.

But the real change is that there are now many cable channels that require payment to the cable systems each month. On these channels, movies are shown. The amount of sex and violence in these movies is beyond belief. TV has become pornography for many channels at many times of the day — pornography of sex and far, far worse, pornography of violence. The amount of callous killing and maiming and cruelty on cable TV goes far beyond the amount of nudity and sex.

W e are in a whole new world where a child can see things on TV (not to mention the Internet) that would have made a sailor blush. This "pornografication" (to invent a word) of TV has happened largely without comment, but its effects must be serious. How did it happen? What's next? Celebrity sex? It is a scary world on the tube now, and I will get into it more in the future. □

Sex and Violence Pervades TV

BEN
STEIN

DREEMZ

I N THE EARLY 1970S, I, YOUR SERVANT, HAD A LITTLE black-and-white Panasonic TV when I lived in a Spartan "preceptor's suite" at College V of the University of California at Santa Cruz. For the first time in my life, I watched a good deal of prime-time TV.

At that time, there were three networks and only crime shows and comedies. I cannot recall all the shows I watched, but *Hawaii Five-O*, *Mannix*, and *The Rockford Files* come to mind, plus the comedies of the day like *Mary Tyler Moore* and *All in the Family*.

I noticed that there were patterns

But I have started watching TV again as I rest up here in Sandpoint, Idaho. And I have noticed a vast, astonishing change in TV.

For one thing, much of TV is what might laughingly be called "reality" shows, i.e., unscripted shows. In these shows, an amazing amount of content is about sex, and a lot is about "cheating" or betrayal in sexual matters. A

TV has become pornography for many channels

truly amazing amount beyond that is about weight and eating. And beyond that, there is a big hunk about buying and selling things — pawnshops, excavations in storage lockers, searching for bargains doing. Tom staggers backward, blinks hard, and attempts to gain clarity. This is not the person he started out to be, not the original person God called to marriage. He may be appalled and taken aback at his own behavior. He may at this point give himself an ultimatum to use the Internet for cybersex no longer. He may be faithful to this vow for one week, two weeks, three weeks, maybe a month. But his resistance can easily fade. His resolve can easily weaken. In a moment of neediness, Tom logs on again and searches out the same familiar Web sites. He rationalizes and tells himself the "scare" was simply a fluke, a mishap. He tells himself that no one is on to him. He believes he can continue. Perhaps he changes screen names or Internet providers, or buys a new computer all together. The prudent fear fades and he feels anonymous again. He takes on the weight of the secret once more. He ventures online until the next time he almost is caught. At some point, Tom will hit the ultimate rock bottom that will land him face to face with the inner work of hope.

THE INNER WORK OF HOPE

No one can do the realization inner work for Tom. His counselor cannot do it nor can his twelve-step group. The practice of the virtues is crucial to healing. The theological virtues of faith, hope, and love, and the cardinal virtues of prudence, justice, fortitude, and temperance are *the* path to healing. Often, Tom believes God will love him only after he somehow fixes himself. In this, he even attempts to build God into his illusion.

When Tom does hit rock bottom, the only thing left to do is to hope. When he hopes, he is *by that very act of hope* united to God. Hope is the first step: "In hope we were saved" (Rom 8:24).

The virtue of hope is the first virtue in the healing process. Hope does not dismiss the present painful circumstances as if to say, "One day I may figure all this out and be free of this difficulty." Hope is not wishing things away or mere optimism. No. Hope is the virtue that leads Tom to look squarely into the obscurity, complexity, and difficulty of the pain. Hope looks to a future good even in the midst of the pain. Hope is the virtue that sustains the Christian in times of difficulty. Coming forth from denial can only take place in hope. One has the strength to *realize* inner pain only in the context of a greater hope. The one who hopes is joined to God by the very act of hope.

In this new freedom, we can choose to forgive those who wounded us. One day, St. Peter asked Jesus how many times we must forgive those who do wrong to us. He asked: "Lord, if my brother sins against me, how often must I forgive him? As many as seven times?" Jesus answered, "I say to you, not seven times, but seventy-seven times" (Matt 18:21–22). Peter wants to limit forgiveness. He proposes what he believes is a good measure: seven times. Numbers in the Bible carry a deep meaning. Seven is the number of completion, of fullness. In the genealogy of the Gospel of Luke, Jesus is the seventy-seventh in the direct line (Luke 3:23–38). There are seven days in the week that God created. There are seven days of the feast of Passover (Exod 13:3–10). There were seven years of plenty and seven years of famine in the dream of Pharaoh (Gen 41). Joshua marches around Jericho seven times, and seven days later, the walls of the city collapse (Josh 6). Jesus speaks seven last words from the cross. There are seven gifts of the Holy Spirit and seven sacraments. In responding to Peter, Jesus takes the number of completeness and takes it even further. He multiplies it by ten and then adds seven more. Ten is the basis of the decimal number system and central to all basic calculations. We have ten fingers. God gave Moses Ten Commandments (Exod 20:1–17; Deut 5:6–21). In his response to Peter about forgiveness, Jesus combines the fullness of ten with the completeness of seven. Our forgiveness must be both full and complete. This means not simply forgiving all slights automatically. The meaning is much deeper. We must *learn to forgive* as a way of life. We must learn to forgive not just repeated faults and wrongs, but we must *forgive the network of pain and wrongs back all the way back*, as far as possible, to its original sources. We forgive not just the wrong our brother does to us, but we forgive the one who harmed our brother to lead him to act in an evil way to us. And so on. We must go all the way back, because only through this persistent forgiveness can we dismantle our elaborate defenses and coping mechanisms of fear and control. As these are dismantled, we can restructure and rebuild, from the basic and strong foundation, an intuitive awareness for grace and the gift of self. Forgiveness leads us to build our house on rock (Matt 7:24–27).

The sober realization of hitting rock bottom leads us to hope. And hope moves us to forgive. Tom experiences God's forgiveness in the sacrament of reconciliation. Through this sacrament, Tom receives the mercy of God and that shows Tom he is an adopted son of God. Again, if we turn to the parable of the Prodigal Son, we see that son's moment of confession after his examination of conscience. He proceeds to his father and tells the truth: "Father, I have sinned against heaven and against you. I no longer deserve to be called your son…" (Luke 15:18–19). Lies have all the consistency of sand. Once Tom has hit the rock bottom of truth, he can begin to build a new foundation. Notice the response of the father. He does not say, "I told you so" or "What did you do with the money?" The father does not glare at his renegade son. The father does not withdraw into passive-aggressive avoidance. As soon as the father hears the son say, "I no longer deserve to be called your son," the father responds, "Quickly, bring the finest robe and put it on him…" (Luke 15:22). The father realizes that the son must not lose his internal sense of his own identity *as a son*.

God the Father does the same for us. We are the adopted sons and daughters of God. What Jesus is by nature, the eternal

Son of God, we are by grace: adopted sons and daughters of God. Restoring our internal sense of being a child of God is the foundation of all subsequent healing, especially in the case of cybersex and Internet pornography. We no longer need to exist in the old network of worldly fear. St. John is speaking about worldly fear when he says, "There is no fear in love, but perfect love drives out fear because fear has to do with punishment, and so one who fears is not yet perfect in love" (1 John 4:18). When we experience the forgiveness and mercy of God, we can begin to understand we are his beloved sons and daughters. We can begin to live in the new world of hope.

THE EXAMINATION OF CONSCIENCE

The examination of conscience follows naturally upon hitting rock bottom and is also the preparation for the sacrament of reconciliation. This is a crucial step in inner work. This work is carried out under the principal rule of being gentle with oneself while being attentive to the patterns, consequences, relapse, and effects of painful and sinful behavior. The examination of conscience is not self-shaming or beating oneself up with accusatory and self-defeating thoughts. In the fifth chapter of the Gospel of St. Luke, as the apostles are fishing, Jesus instructs Simon Peter to let down the nets for a catch. Simon Peter does so. St. Ambrose, commented on this passage and said, "Nets do not destroy those that they catch, but save them and draw them upwards from the depths to the light; bringing those who are wavering, from the knowledge of the lowest things to the knowledge of the highest."[3]

The examination of conscience means living our daily life with a deeper attentiveness to the way we act. It means taking time at the end of the day, and even at key times during the day, to review our relationships and actions. It uncovers the hidden ways our negative thinking leads to painful feelings and then on to inappropriate and sinful behavior. Tom's recovery and healing consists, in part, in awareness and vigilance over his daily circumstances. This awareness and vigilance help Tom in the struggle to avoid the occasion of sin and respond to temptation with virtue. The fathers of early desert monasticism maintained the one who would grow in the spiritual life must maintain vigilance and awareness over one's thoughts.

Tom can learn to examine his conscience in a more mature way. Learning to be accountable and honest with oneself, others, and God is the ongoing task at every stage of inner work. The examination of conscience begins the preparation for the sacrament of reconciliation and is the regular means by which we can be transparent and accountable for our actions. Guilt is different from shame. Shame is about *who I am* as a person, and it is never healthy. Guilt is about *what I do*, and guilt can be very healthy. Guilt is *not* a guilt-trip. It is a signal, a summons to relevant accountability and willingness to take responsibility for one's painful behavior. Guilt does not approve of the acting out behavior. It does not dismiss the evil that has been done. Healthy guilt is not self-centered, but seeks mature and grace-filled ways to undermine the negative thinking that reinforces the behavior. This takes time.

THE OCCASION OF SIN

I remember when I was an acolyte in the seminary. I was assigned for ten weeks to parish ministry over the summer. One evening I accompanied the pastor to the wake service of a parishioner who had passed away. The pastor was to lead the service, and I was to offer a brief reflection on the gospel reading. As we left the rectory, the pastor tossed me the keys to his gray, four-door Mercury with a V-8 engine. I had never driven a car with anything more than four cylinders. As we drove the rural roads, I pressed the gas pedal. I was so taken with the speed and handling of the vehicle that I must have thought the stop sign was optional. The car approaching the crossroad had no stop sign. We missed by inches as I veered into the thankfully empty oncoming lane to avoid a disaster. At the height of the almost catastrophe, the pastor called out, "God sorry sins!" After the near-miss, as we went to four-cylinder speed, I asked him what "God sorry sins!" meant. He replied that it was the Act of Contrition...the short form! In the Act of Contrition we pray that the Lord protect us from the near occasion of sin. With many sins, as with those against chastity, we also benefit from protection from the proximate and remote occasion of sin.

Tom's old patterns of sin, faults, and habits must yield to the new grace-filled ways of belief and thinking. His temptation to use Internet pornography does not begin when he is sitting at the computer. It begins hours, if not days, earlier. As Tom learns to examine his conscience, he can more readily identify when he is feeling adrift, insecure, over-tired, over-worked, stressed, or lonely. He can identify when he tries to be the hero, and how quickly after these futile attempts, he feels lonely. These feelings, along with continued internal worry and preoccupation about his status, would easily wear him down, exhaust his inner resources, and make him more vulnerable to acting out in a virtual world rather than suffer in the real one. He can be whoever he wants to be online. For many, the virtual world is not a hobby but a second life. Tom would escape into fantasy and hide in a compartmentalized virtual world as a routine defense against the pressures of loneliness, pleasing, super-activity, anger, boredom, insecurity, and exhaustion. As Tom learns to identify the risk factors and early onset of these feelings, and to call upon creative and life-giving ways to redirect and counter the effects of these experiences, he grows in the life of virtue.

A FOOTHOLD

Tom was taught as a young child to approach the sacrament of reconciliation for the forgiveness of sins. Unfortunately, he has drifted from that practice in later years. As he encounters sinful situations in life, the Holy Spirit continues to urge Tom to approach the mercy of God so he may be forgiven and strengthened in virtue. The use of Internet pornography wounds the dignity of the human person, harms the sanctity of human sexuality, and is always a matter of serious sin.

Tom may discover his turn to Internet pornography involves various factors. Fear, force, habit, strong emotion, immaturity, and anxiety may condition his actions as he engages in cybersex. It is important for Tom to understand the way in which these factors affect his behavior. The first edition of the *Catechism of the Catholic Church*, published in 1994, specifically noted sins against chastity might be influenced by "affective immaturity, force of acquired habit, conditions of anxiety, or other psychological or social factors that lessen, or even extenuate moral culpability."[4] The second edition of the *Catechism*, published in 1997, includes a significant modification. The second edition states sins against chastity may be influenced by "affective immaturity, force of acquired habit, conditions of anxiety, or other psychological or social factors that *can* lessen, or even *reduce to a minimum*, moral culpability" (emphasis added). Note that the second edition states that the factors "*can* lessen" but it is not immediately presumed that they do, and that *if* they do lessen moral culpability, they lessen only to the extent that they reduce it to a minimum, not extenuate it completely. It is true that his culpability may lessen due to an undue influence from these factors. Even though the use may be a habit for Tom, and thus diminishes his sufficient reflection and full consent of the will, the action itself always remains serious and it is crucial that it be confessed in the sacrament of reconciliation.

The gauging of moral responsibility is a sober and solemn task. The discovery of Tom's minimal rather than extenuated responsibility is not some way of making him feel ashamed or bad because of what he has done. It is actually quite hopeful. Even under the duress of the pattern of sin he can find responsibility, that is, *the ability to respond*. He is not destined or fated to perform these actions, nor is he excused completely.

The assessment of culpability is not just a determination of how much Tom has sinned; it is also a decisive step toward responsibility for being well.[5] The modifiers of responsibility, such as habit, strong emotion, or immaturity, are not only assertions that a person may have minimal culpability, but a strong affirmation that a person retains a measure of freedom. If a person was exhausted of all responsibility for his or her actions, then how would he or she ever truly approach God and change? If Tom is aware of even the minimum of culpability, then he has a responsibility to engage realistic steps to remedy that culpability by prudent discussion with a confessor and/or spiritual director. Tom also has a responsibility, based on awareness of even a minimum of culpability, to take attendant steps such as meeting with a perceptive counselor, and judicious engagement of a twelve-step program, building in objective measures of accountability through support groups, faithfulness to weekly and perhaps daily systems of accountability. Our Holy Father Pope Benedict XVI praised the work of such groups during his historic apostolic visit to Brazil in 2007. On that journey, the Holy Father met with a community named *Nossa Senhora da Glória*, which is also known as *Fazenda da Esperança*, or, the Farm of Hope. The *Fazenda da Esperança* serves those who suffer from addiction. On that occasion, the Holy Father expressed his deep appreciation for, in his words, "those many other institutions throughout the world which work to rebuild and renew the lives of these brothers and sisters of ours present in our midst, who God loves with a preferential love. I am thinking of groups such as Alcoholics Anonymous and Narcotics Anonymous as well as the sobriety associations working generously in many communities so as to build up the lives of others."[6]

Even apparently incidental healing measures may grow from Tom's examination of conscience: the installation of a glass window on his office door with the computer screen fully visible and the installation of blocking systems with safety software and filters on his computer and iPhone. Prevention and intervention are not mere options. They can be lifesavers and marriage savers.

The determination that the person was acting with diminished culpability is not a carte blanche to continue the serious behavior. On the contrary, the person is required to seek the healing means of grace all the more. It appears that Tom's actions were carried out in rapid succession over a short period of time. It seems the near occasion of sin came on him as an avalanche. But on second look, after examining his conscience, Tom can see he had many choices. Tom's indulgence in cybersex is directly related not only to his frustration or amount of sexual tension on any given day, but to a series of shortages in the past two weeks: his lack of a day off, his righteous workaholism and resentment, his missing times of prayer, his failure to have outlet with friends, the mounting demands of his perfectionist style, both personally and professionally. Every deficit seeks an indulgence eventually.

The sexual appetite is not insurmountable or so unwieldy that it cannot be integrated. Such integration necessarily begins with the strategic intersection and interaction of the freedom of the person, his or her appetites, and the grace and love of God. If Tom had acted responsibly, even in minimal fashion toward healthy renewals, outlets, and styles of life, then the stop-gaps in the near occasion of sin would have been footholds where grace can plant a tree, or a cross, which the next time might break his fall and save him.

APPROACHING CONFESSION

Tom, like many who use Internet pornography, senses the desire to go to confession. Often enough, it can be lack of understanding or fear that delays Tom's approaching the sacrament of reconciliation. He might not know when or where confessions are heard…he might forget "how" to go to confession…he might feel awkward, like if he stands in line everyone will know what he did wrong…he might fear that the priest will recognize his voice and think badly of him for his sin. This is simply not true. The Pharisees complain that Jesus "welcomes sinners and eats with them" (Luke 15:2).

The times for the sacrament of reconciliation are ordinarily published on the cover of the church bulletin at the local parish. If it has been a long time since Tom has approached the sacrament of reconciliation, the best thing to do is to let the priest know. The priest welcomes Tom warmly and leads him through how to go to confession. Tom may make the decision to remain anonymous or approach face-to-face. Basically, Tom, after examining his conscience, that is, reflecting on what sins he has committed, goes to the reconciliation room or confessional area of the church at the time confessions are heard, approaches when the priest is available, begins with the Sign of the Cross, hears a welcome from the priest and perhaps a Scripture reading. The priest then invites Tom to confess his sins. The priest is always ready to provide assistance to lead Tom through the celebration of the sacrament of reconciliation.

It is very helpful to keep two images in mind as we approach the sacrament of reconciliation. The first is that of the scriptural account of the Prodigal Son. The second is of the woman who is caught in the act of adultery and is brought to Jesus. These accounts reveal that Jesus is always merciful to the sinner who seeks forgiveness. The confession of sins, the sorrow, and the willingness to perform a penance, that is, an act by which the penitent manifests his or her renewal and dedication to make amends for sin through the new life of grace, are all important steps of healing.

The priest, through the power of the Church, absolves us of our sins. This brings the grace and mercy of God to the depths of our souls. Sanctifying grace is the grace of Jesus Christ that comes to us by the action of the Holy Spirit in and through the Church, most especially in the Sacraments. Sanctifying grace brings the Trinity to dwell in our soul. Through this grace, the Holy Spirit conforms and configures us to Jesus Christ. Grace is not magical or automatic. If we are looking for results or trying to gauge progress, we will inevitably end up focusing on the puzzle of ourselves rather than on the mystery of Jesus. Our part is to approach the action of God with a faithful disposition and a humble anticipation as we invite Him to dwell within us. This indwelling is accompanied by a glimpse of God that convinces us of his love at deep levels of our being—levels of which we were previously only dimly aware. Doubt dissolves through grace. We are led to trust God's absence as much as his presence. We sense a heritage and a direction within our reach. The unity and nearness to God transform us. His love is at once simple and incomprehensible.

The confession, contrition, satisfaction, and absolution essential to the sacrament of reconciliation are not a list of rules or hoops that one must jump through. They are not an obstacle course we must complete to somehow earn forgiveness. Forgiveness cannot be earned; it is only and always a gift. The acts of the penitent and absolution are postures of healing. Going to Confession is not just "going through the motions." Going to Confession is not a motion or a gesture. It is a purposeful action. Confession is a place to humbly acknowledge the feelings of inadequacy and self-centeredness that often underlie our sins. Humility is the central guide to confession. It is not easy to be honest and candid about our weaknesses, and to confront our guilt. Yet, this is the path to healing and to emerging from the cycle of pain that reinforces patterns of sin. The trust and transparency of the truth is not easy, but it is life-giving.

FORGIVENESS

Forgiveness takes place in a community, that is, a communion of persons. In the sacrament of reconciliation, the priest and penitent form a community into which the mercy and love of God the Father are bestowed as the Holy Spirit makes effective the merits and fruits of the sacrifice of Jesus on the cross. Tom's journey to healing must be founded on the cross of Jesus. On the cross, Jesus experienced all of the hurt, abuse, neglect, and violence of history: that of every death camp and torture chamber, of every war and abortion, of every abuse and domestic violence, of every addiction and betrayal, of every criminal act, and all the pain and suffering man could experience. Jesus bore it all—and underneath it all, he loved us. The crucifix can never be far from those involved in healing from Internet pornography. Whether it be at the end of a rosary in a pocket, or on a bedroom, home, or office wall, the crucifix is a reminder of suffering love that must always be near. The crucifix is not magic. It is far more. It reminds us we are not alone, and that we are loved. The Blessed Virgin Mary and the beloved disciple stood at the foot of the cross. We must, in every pain we experience, insert ourselves consciously into that community at the foot of the cross. There, we unite ourselves with Jesus, and through him, with all those who have suffered in every time and place. We join there, at the cross, the ranks of those who do not pretend anymore, who do not believe in magic, but hold fast to love. We, when we hold the crucifix, can feel the strength of this love. The alienation of Internet pornography is countered by the participation in the communal and sacramental life of the Church.

The mercy one experiences in the sacrament of reconciliation leads to the virtue of love. Pope John Paul II said mercy is the second name of love.[7] Mercy heals the wound of sin and strengthens us to resist further sin. Forgiveness changes our heart. Thankfully, forgiveness is not automatic. Forgiveness is the opposite of magic. It is the opposite of a quick, instantaneous, satisfying illusion. Forgiveness is a meaningful, prolonged, fulfilling reality. It is not an abstract or naïve wave of the hand that remotely dismisses guilt. Forgiveness means to *give as before*, to give with all the original and spontaneous depth of love that was present before the wound. To forgive means to love from a new place: to love even from within the wound. This love creates new life out of the distance caused by pain. Forgiveness does not mean we go back and put ourselves in the position to be victimized or hurt again. It means we have come to a new place where we choose to love even in the most distant and alienated of hurts. Forgiveness is not a feeling conjured up. It emerges from mercy, and mercy comes forth from love.

Living the life of virtue helps Tom to see clearly that pornography always treats the human being as an object that one seeks to possess. Technology, too, can lead us to treat persons as objects. We get used to getting what we want immediately when we push the buttons on the cable remote control or computer keyboard. Soon, we begin to treat people as objects, as if we had them under remote control and they should respond to our every need as if at the press of a button. There is no room for love where the person is reduced to the level of an object. In Internet pornography, love, too, is always reduced simply to sex. Divorced from married love, sex loses its proper coordinate and is abridged simply to being a random act. In such a setting, the act itself is also distorted, however, and is reduced simply to a quantitative measure of the experience of pleasure. Pornography absorbs and preoccupies the user in such a way that the senses are dulled and the nuptial meaning of the body is distorted.

The one who sins against chastity necessarily turns in on the self, and is isolated from the other. Blessed Pope John Paul II indicates that sins against chastity have at least nine progressive effects on the person.[8] The user is caught in disordered self-love, rather than authentic love. Looked at in this way, we can say (1) the deepest voice of conscience is suffocated. When conscience is stifled, (2) restlessness results and (3) the inner man is reduced to silence. His activities, therefore, focus more and more on (4) the satisfaction of the senses. This serves (5) to inflame his desire all the more and (6) occupy his will. The pursuit of pleasure becomes the priority, while conscience and the voice of reason grow more and more distant. Our needs can appear to be so intense that they seem to overcome common sense. The self then begins to be consumed in the volley between pride, excuses, and pleasure. Yet, the pleasure brings no authentic relief. (7) The internal resources of the person grow more and more blunted, including the ability to be reflective. What began as attempts under the guise of recreation or entertainment have so distorted the meaning of the inherent capacities of life and love that the (8) self is worn out and (9) the person is exhausted. In this pattern, human sexuality is reduced to being the satisfaction and alleviation of one's own personal erotic need. It is understood as a demand, a requirement, and an entitlement rather than as a gift.

TELLING OUR SECRETS

The Gospel of St. Mark recounts the healing by Jesus of a woman who was afflicted with hemorrhages for twelve years who suffered greatly at the hands of many doctors (Mark 5:25–34). She approaches Jesus to simply touch him, with confidence that if she does so she will be healed. In the midst of the great crowd she reaches out anonymously to touch Jesus. As the woman touches Jesus, her symptoms disappear and she feels as if she has been healed. Jesus feels the power go forth from him, but there is more to the account.

After she is healed, the Gospel tells us Jesus, aware that healing has gone forth from him, asks who it was that has touched him in the midst of this crowd. Then, the woman "approached [Jesus] in fear and trembling. She fell down before Jesus and told him the whole truth" (Mark 5:33). Notice that the woman tells Jesus "the whole truth." It is at this point the healing is complete, as Jesus says to her: "Daughter, your faith has saved you. Go in peace and be cured of your affliction" (Mark 5:34).[9]

The virtue of hope leads Tom to rediscover his worth as a son of God. From this comes the strength to realize that if Tom himself is a son of God, then so are persons around Tom. In fact, if we are all sons and daughters of God, then we are all brothers and sisters to one another. Here we see the basis for Jesus' command to love our neighbor (Mark 12:31; John 13:34; Luke 10:27–28). Being a son of God does not mean that Tom can engage in any behavior he likes and that God is a pushover. This would mean that faith would grant license for all kinds of behavior. Instead, Tom learns his actions have meaning and express his person. He realizes the people who are portrayed in pornographic images are also children of God. They are Tom's brothers and sisters. He must treat them with justice, and not use their images of their bodies for his own pleasure. Loving our neighbor means treating them with justice. The virtue of justice means giving another their due, and not treating their bodies, or the images of their bodies, merely as things.

As the old saying goes, "We are as sick as our secrets." Telling our secrets helps to dispel their power over us. Healing involves returning, as the adult I am now, to those old pathways. In order to find our original spontaneity, we must allow the Holy Spirit to guide us in healing back to the moment in our lives before love was turned into fear. As the prophet Jeremiah says,

"Thus says the LORD: Stand beside the earliest roads, ask the pathways of old which is the way to good, and walk it; thus you will find rest for your souls" (Jer 6:16).

Unburdened from our secrets, we are free to treat others with justice. But telling our secrets is never easy. It requires the help of two other virtues: the virtues of fortitude and prudence. Fortitude is the courage to face and overcome obstacles that stand between us and the authentic good. Prudence means learning the nature of the difficulties we face and facing them with honesty and accountability. The courage that comes with fortitude strengthens Tom to admit the inner thoughts, justifications, feelings, demands, complaints, behaviors, and patterns that he has hidden for so long. Tom must admit the times when he has cut corners, made excuses, and lied. Doing this, he risks telling the truth and showing his wounds. Tom did not even fully realize he had secrets until the light was cast into the corners of his life, and this light made him feel a new warmth and see a new direction.

As this strength gathers, Tom finds that in moments of temptation, as the conflict heightens, God seeks to strengthen him. God does not override Tom's own strength to make Tom walk away from temptation as if he were a robot. God helps Tom to overcome his own fears, to grow in confidence, to appreciate the small victories, to persist even when he suffers, and to remain humble. For example, if Tom is watching a movie, and he sees that the scene is progressing to a plot line that tends to push his sexual buttons, hope tells him there is more to life than this. As he hears this message, he begins to discover a new way forward. Prudence and fortitude plead with Tom to turn the movie off or to get up and leave the theater. Tom leaves not because he is weak, but because he is strong: strong enough to treat others with justice, and therefore refuse to be led to use the image of another person, or his own body, as a thing for self-centered pleasure.

Fortitude gives Tom the strength to look both at his behavior and to its roots, and to share his secrets in healthy places, rather than to seek out unhealthy places. Prudence is the virtue that leads Tom to choose well and to act reasonably in the concrete situations of daily life. Fortitude and prudence come together to guide Tom to do what is truly good, even in the small details of the present moment. The woman from the Gospel of St. Mark approaches Jesus in fear and trembling. Even though she was already healed of the physical symptoms, there was a deeper healing. We do not know "the whole truth" she told Jesus. But we do know that after she does so she is not only healed of the symptoms, but that Jesus announces her as a *daughter* who has not only been healed, but *saved*.

The same is true for the Samaritan woman. Jesus saves her from her secrets. He speaks to her of the many husbands she has had. Her many failed relationships were very embarrassing for this woman. Were her patterns the result of a deeper pain in her life? Did she have secrets that were a source of shame for her? Jesus frees her from her secrets by speaking with her about them, so much so that she now *announces* her secrets to the town: "Come see a man who told me everything I have done" (John 4:29). Imagine, this is the same woman who avoided the crowd from the town. She would go to the well at the hottest time of the day so as not to endure their glares and gossip. And here she is *announcing* herself right in their midst and making reference to her past. Now, she is free. She is freer than any other resident of that town, because she has met Jesus, and he has given her the gift of living water—the life of virtue. The conversation with Jesus took place at a well. Now, thanks to the water of life given to her by Jesus, *she has become the well* for the people in that town...she *evangelizes* the town: "Many of the Samaritans of that town began to believe in him because of the word of the woman who testified, 'He told me everything I have done'"

(John 4:39). That same gift of living water is available to Tom, and to us as well.

It is important for Tom to realize his secrets, even the painful ones, need to be reverenced and honored. Secrets, especially early on in Tom's healing, are not to be shared indiscriminately and haphazardly. Tom should disclose his secrets only where they will be held in confidence, as with a prudent confessor and spiritual director, and perhaps a discreet and knowledgeable counselor. It might be the case that early in his healing process, Tom experiences enthusiasm with telling his secrets. He might even get mileage out of the attention that comes from sharing his secrets. Once he has been received well by a director or counselor, he might be tempted to rush ahead and begin to speak about painful experiences with friends and acquaintances. His friends, as good as they are, may very well not be able to handle too much personal information too early.

HEALING, NOT FIXING

The ghosts that haunt us in the form of our pain can be laid to rest. In fact, they can point us to healing. Our distressing memories want to be healed. One way to heal is to get the venom that causes the pain out: to talk out the old pain in a new safe place. Talking out the pain helps the healing. The old saying goes, "If you can't feel it, you can't heal it." Very often, in our first attempts at healing, we get in our own way. So often we demand the next external good feeling to *fix* the pain or deficit inside us. We want our life fixed. But life cannot be fixed. Life can only be *healed*. We often spend a great deal of energy attempting to *fix* ourselves rather than *be* ourselves. The quicker the fix, the longer the pain. To be healed, losses and wounds must be *grieved*. Grieving takes time.[10] It requires learning to feel again. Feeling was so painful, for so long, that many stopped long ago, substituting thinking for feeling. There is no preempting or short-cutting around feelings. Feelings are facts and they want to be honored. The only way out is through. Restructuring establishes new, appropriate, and life-giving beliefs, thoughts, and behaviors that open original and holy ways to authentic patterns of life.

Our attempts to fix ourselves are often known only to a small number of people. Thank God. We would not want anyone thinking we were somehow imperfect. We read self-help books to find out why we get angry so easily. We watch talk shows to try to learn tips that will finally fix our family hurts. These measures are short-lived. We still hide in our moods *for hours* and in our patterns for *years*. A friend of mine recently explained how he put so many hours into a high-profile project at work. For several months, he came into the office early and stayed late. He worked weekends. He constantly monitored and tracked the ups and downs of the market. The deadline approached. He prepared the final draft, double-checked and triple-checked from every angle, only to have his boss ridicule a minor, inconsequential detail of the final proposal in front of his colleagues and co-workers. His getting angry at his boss would have been as bad as the boss's poor form in ridiculing him. He could have gotten angry when he was away from the office and in a safe place. But he didn't.

He has learned the rule. He keeps it more surely than most of the Ten Commandments: "Don't get angry…especially in front of the boss." So, the anger gets swallowed, even after he leaves the office: "I wasn't angry." If he could have seen himself, he would have seen his lips tighten and brow furrow. His body knew he was angry. That which we repress does not go away; it becomes, ironically, an obsession. He insists, "No…I wasn't angry. That just happens. That's the way the business world is…Besides I should have caught it earlier."

He has gone from swallowing anger he did not like to gulping down self-criticism that he tells himself is proper. Seven hours later, when he pulls into the driveway, the anger seethes to the surface. Not at his boss though, but at the kids, the home-work, the teacher who assigned the homework, the double-parked neighbor, or his wife. He does not show his anger directly to his boss, co-workers, and neighbors who often spark it in him. But he does show it to his family and friends when they are sim-ply being themselves. His boss can fire him. The kids can't.

So later that night, when he has a moment alone, he thinks back: "Why was today so *hard?* Work dragged on and on." "And then, why did I get so mad that the homework wasn't done…that practice ran late…?" The day dragged on at work because he was carrying the boulder of anger his boss had handed off to him. And he handed it off to his family, in the form of an unbalanced, insecure emotional response, rather than disposing of it in a safe place. He tolerates himself and attempts to control others so that there will be no more pain, rejection, or hurt. He routinely discounts his blessings and magnifies his faults. He thinks *he is* the mistakes he has made. He forgets that in his deepest mistake, *he is never a mistake.* His first step to authentic love is to learn to trust again. The shame and blame patterns of early rejections sabotage the path to love. The pattern is familiar to all of us that when we *need* the assistance of healthy anger, we order it away from us and it grows to be a burden of internalized hostility that weighs us down. Then, we unleash it on an innocent bystander.

Again, consider Tom in the story at the beginning of this book. If we were to learn more about his inner life and his secrets, we would discover that Tom believes he must always be the top performer in his area. His perfectionist efforts build an incredible deficit in his personal life. He suffers from the stress of having to always be number one, to outdo his colleagues and the competition, to maintain long-distance relationships. Sooner or later, this lifestyle of perfectionism and control takes its toll.

As a recompense or release, he must have one area where he is not perfect…not in control. The pressure builds up and he seeks release, often in a quick and available way, and in a method that can access the deepest appetites so that the effects of the relief are pervasive through his entire system. Internet pornography appears to fit the bill.

When daily life does not turn out as we plan, and our imperfections are coming to the surface, we send out the troops: The platoon of anger marches forth to scare others away from our weaknesses. We would make very good spies. We hide things well, and for a long period of time. To the larger number of people, we like to present ourselves as having "it" all together, but much of our daily life is really cover-ups. That is to say, we pretend. We pretend we came from the perfect family, got good grades, were the most popular person in high school, were onto the latest trends, and had parents who got along. We now act as if this is the career we planned for all along. We keep our daily difficulties, missed opportunities, mistakes, and disappointments rather secret. We might even feel embarrassed about our struggles. We have our "acceptable side" and our "unacceptable side." As a result, we often find ourselves living in two worlds. Ironically, we spend a lot of energy doing the things in the one world as a way to fix, or compensate for, the unacceptable things in the other world. The world we do not accept is where we put what we find less than acceptable. Under such circumstances, our inner life can seem like a Ponzi scheme. Our early walls, built to protect us, persist into adulthood and deter us from healthy and holy relationships.

GUIDANCE TO THE GIFT

The world does not know what to do with a gift. If you cannot buy it, deserve it, earn it, count it, win it, own it, control it, measure it, weaken it, advertise it, or make money from it, then the world does not know what to do with it. Internet pornography thrives on self-centeredness, isolation, and deception. One cannot conquer Internet pornography simply through the determination of an iron will, the insistence of clenched teeth, and the resolve of white-knuckled grit alone. One must be ready to find a prudent, knowledgeable, and experienced guide with whom one can be ruthlessly truthful about the self, about one's patterns, deceptions, short cuts, and ambiguities. This guide cannot simply be a family member or friend. It must be someone who has the professional distance and the knowledge to care in a free and mature manner. This would take place in a professional setting with a regular appointment time and proper boundaries. This guide must also know the path. They must be familiar with the human condition, the gifts of God and the pitfalls and perils of recovery from Internet pornography. Regularly meeting with a seasoned guide, along with the assistance of a support group, helps achieve full accountability. The false belief that one can escape the perils of Internet pornography on one's own is simply another version of the false self-sufficiency that fuels the pornography problem in the first place. Asking for help is the first sign of authentic strength. The guide must also be able to offer assistance in looking to the causes of Internet pornography use.

Telling his secrets is not a one-time thing for Tom. He must have a regular, safe, and trustworthy relationship with the one who guides him. A consistent and committed professional relationship must emerge by which he tells all the secrets that have led to his behavior.[11] This is because inner healing is a lot like recovering from a stomach virus. At some point, we wake up and sense the compelling need to be sick. We rise and go to the washroom, and then we feel better and lie down again. The sick feeling returns within 20 minutes and then we rise again. This process continues until we begin to stabilize. The same is true with our inner pain.

We must purge the poisons if the healing is to begin in earnest. Tom will learn the old nemesis of control will rear its head again and again in this process. He will want to be the one in charge, to manage the outcome, to control the conversation. Tom must surrender this drive and be faithful to the truth behind the process.

The water the Samaritan woman asks for is the water of truth. At first, she does not understand the full meaning of truth. She envisions the water as something that will enable her to not have to keep making the cumbersome trip to the well. But Jesus, through his conversation with her, introduces to her the true meaning of the water of grace he provides through the action of the Holy Spirit.

As Tom continues his recovery and healing, he begins to open new doors. After Tom hits rock bottom, he has the opportunity to embark on the inner work of hope. He learns to examine his conscience, and discovers the importance of meeting with a wise counselor and spiritual director, as well as working with a support group. Above all, the sacrament of reconciliation reveals the mercy of God for Tom. From the experience, Tom gains the strength to begin to tell his secrets and to grow in the life of grace and virtue. This is all part of the inner work of conversion. Through telling his secrets, Tom uncovers the negative beliefs, thought processes, and attitudes that enabled or reinforced the acting out through Internet pornography.

HONESTY, TRANSPARENCY, AND ACCOUNTABILITY

We can often believe that even our best intentions and repeated efforts to live a good and holy life are in vain. So many find that even though they try as they might, they keep falling back into the old ways of sin. It seems to them that no matter how many good decisions they muster up or firm resolutions they make, these seem so short lived, and the person eventually returns to the same sins. Tom can sometimes feel like a hypocrite, even as he attempts to escape the cycle of cybersex. Like so many who struggle with this battle, the sense of shame and isolation grows. It seems his efforts to live the moral life are a useless facade. He wonders why he continues to try. Some who make the initial steps to healing, unfortunately, give up in the face of repeated failures. It is important to recall that the internalization of virtue is not automatic. The life of virtue is the result of the work of the Holy Spirit as his gifts move upon our docility and trust. The *Catechism of the Catholic Church* teaches: "Self-mastery is long and exacting work. One can never consider it acquired once and for all. It presupposes renewed effort at all stages of life. The effort required can be more intense in certain periods, such as when the personality is being formed during childhood and adolescence."[12]

Tom may experience relapse, binging, and setbacks. The key at these moments is the return to the life of grace, together with his own honesty, transparency, and accountability, which also come through the virtues of hope, justice, fortitude, and prudence. He may discover that hanging out with the same old crowd puts him in the occasion of sin. The old ways of speaking about women and their bodies do not prove masculinity, just insecurity. He may learn his tenacious resolve to be the best is what sets him on a downward defeating spiral where he ends up doing his worst. He may begin to understand that PG-13 and R-rated movies, although not technically pornographic, can easily trigger his urges by the portrayal of highly suggestive situations and scenes. The trigger seeks to recall the pleasurable sense experience. The same may be true of spam e-mail with highly sexualized words in the subject line. He may discover patterns in his life he never before detected. He may do many things for speed and comfort: The way he relates to work, family, entertainment,

friends, and vacation may all be about quick comforts. His diet
may be geared to fast food and comfort food. He may find that
he always seems to be standing in front of screens, buttons, and
lists: the television, the computer, the ATM, the microwave
oven, or the cell phone, BlackBerry, or iPod. All of these screens
purport to deliver immediate *satisfaction*. Tom must avoid these
screens and turn to another screen. Tom will only be *fulfilled*
when he goes before the confessional screen. The key question
he needs to ask is: "Why do I need comfort and satisfaction so
quickly and so often?"

CHAPTER 5

"SIR, GIVE ME THIS WATER"
(JOHN 4:15)

THE TURN TO HEALING

Where do persons who struggle with pornography turn for healing? Where does Tom turn? He must turn back to the face—to the face of Jesus Christ. This turn consists in the transformation from fear into love, from love into the gift: the gift of self. The Church teaches man can only find himself by a sincere gift of self.[1] This is a paradox. The only way the human person can be fulfilled in the interior is by offering himself as a gift to others. Being a gift of self is not mere volunteerism or pleasing of others. A true and authentic gift of self emerges only from the transformation that emerges when one looks upon the face of Jesus Christ—when one faces beauty instead of self-centeredness.

It can be hard to find the way to Jesus. When we look for a life-giving direction, the world constantly throws up a mirror in our path: "What will other people think?" "Do I fit in?" "If only I sounded smarter." "If only I were more popular, then everything would be OK." "If only we had more money then I'd make my mark." Tom is like us. He needs help to find the way to Jesus. This help comes from only one place, or, rather, one *Person*: the Holy Spirit. The Holy Spirit works in the Church and gives us his gifts so that we have the strength to follow Jesus and slip away from the false ways of the world.

LEANING ON JESUS

Tom learns that even though the urge to act out via online pornography is strong, there is another action that is always stronger: the sufferings of Jesus Christ. Tom can learn to allow Jesus to be his strength. Just as the cross of Jesus is central to the sacrament of reconciliation, so too, the self-gift of Jesus on the cross brings grace and virtue to Tom through the Eucharist. Spirituality is not a piling up of practices, but the meeting of a Person, Jesus Christ, in and through his Church. We look on the face of Jesus when we go to Mass.

Attendance at Mass on Sunday or the Vigil Mass on Saturday evening in anticipation of Sunday is central to healing and the new life of grace. The goal is not to be self-focused when we attend Mass, but to be focused on God and his action in our lives. As Tom attends Mass, he may experience guilt feelings, distractions, a sense of unworthiness, or he may feel like a spectator, and feel uninvolved. He may be very poor at keeping a schedule, and he may arrive chronically late. The key is that Tom realizes that being there is crucial for him. At Mass, he comes together with a community, hears the Word of God proclaimed, can receive the Eucharist, and can find effective preaching and catechesis. The virtue of faith is strengthened in each of these moments. This forms the basis for Tom's ongoing inner work. Tom should listen for key words in the Mass that touch him. This is part of healing painful memories and the rebuilding of good memories. He must recall continuously that as we worship God, we are allowing God to work in us. God does not just fix us, he heals us, and healing takes time. Love takes time.

EUCHARISTIC ADORATION

The celebration of Mass is the center of the Church's life. The Blessed Sacrament is reserved after Mass for communion for the sick and those close to death, and also for reverential adoration. The Lord Jesus is sacramentally present in the Eucharist. Many parishes have periods of exposition and benediction of the Blessed Sacrament, which are specific times for prayer before our Lord in the Eucharist. A number of parishes have time and space set aside for perpetual adoration of the Blessed Sacrament. Ordinarily, this takes place in the church building itself or in a chapel. The Eucharist, consecrated at Mass, is placed in the monstrance for adoration. Eucharistic adoration flows from and leads back to the celebration of Mass itself. It is an opportunity, in close proximity to the sacramental presence of the Lord, to rest in his presence, to worship and adore him in silence, and to pray.

When I was an altar boy, there would be exposition of the Blessed Sacrament on Friday afternoons. Two altar boys would be assigned to a half-hour adoration period in church. This meant that, during the school year, altar boys were permitted to be absent from class for a half hour to go to church. We would leave the classroom, vest in a cassock and surplice, and go into the sanctuary of the church where there were two chairs and two kneelers. The half hour seemed very long. I would begin by kneeling, and then sit for a while; then I would read the small prayer book that was left on the shelf of the kneeler and I would look around the church. Sometimes the church would be entirely empty. At that point, there would still be twenty or so minutes left in the half hour! Then, sometimes alone, I would look up at the Eucharist in the monstrance. And I would simply realize that this was God: the one who created the universe, who took flesh and was born of the Virgin Mary, who lived the hidden life at Nazareth, and who performed the miracles. This was *him*: his presence, the one who suffered and died on the cross and rose again. This was *him*. And I was so close to him for these moments. And with that, two altar boys would come to the sanctuary to take the next half hour. The half hour was over. God had taken me into his own time, and the time passed so quickly. I believe these moments grounded my call to the priesthood, and I know that they still ground my life.

Outside of formal times of Eucharistic exposition, many churches are open throughout the day so that the faithful may pray before the presence of Christ in the tabernacle. Eucharistic adoration is an opportunity to take time aside and be in the presence of the One who heals us. Whatever time one can spend in his presence is effective and instrumental to our sanctification and healing. It may be five, ten, or fifteen minutes, or perhaps longer. These moments can set the stage for our day. There are enough churches that offer perpetual adoration that we should be able to find one close enough to be compatible with our daily route and schedule.

In the presence of the Lord we can slow down, take a deep breath, and recenter ourselves before God, the one who has created us, redeemed us, and who strengthens us. We step away from our busy lives and activity of the world to return to the center: the Lord Jesus, who works in the deep places of our heart through the Holy Spirit, so that we may learn the way to the Father.

It is in prayer where Tom's inner work is made fruitful. Tom must learn a new Word to replace all the old words of painful experiences and the toxic culture. This new word can ultimately only be spoken by God. The Son of God, Jesus Christ, the second Person of the Blessed Trinity, is the Word of the God who is always new, and who alone can free us from sin and its effects. The virtue of faith builds on the work begun through the virtues of hope, justice, fortitude, and prudence. The virtue of faith, through the Holy Spirit's gifts of knowledge and understanding, along with effective preaching and teaching, helps Tom to internalize these truths so as to live by them. The knowledge and under-standing that come from faith actually communicate something to the depths of our heart. Through faith, the mysteries of Jesus become alive in us in such a way that we do not simply know *about* God, but that we *know* God. We begin, through the knowledge of faith, to *resemble* the God who dwells in us by grace.

We hear the Word proclaimed in the Church through Sacred Scripture. The one who is recovering from Internet pornography use must become familiar with the Word of God. An easy-to-carry copy of the Bible allows Tom to read accounts of how God has helped and forgiven others who were in difficult situations. This must be a regular source of strength. The Bible can never be far away. Tom can carry it with him, read it for five minutes at the end of lunch hour. Verses of Scripture can serve as a reminder to Tom that strength is made perfect in weakness and that nothing is beyond the grace of God. Tom can imagine himself as the one who is cared for by the Good Samaritan (Luke 10:29–37). Tom can learn the short, powerful verses of the Psalms, which he can call upon in moments of weakness:[2]

> But you, LORD, do not stay far off;
>> my strength, come quickly to help me." (Ps 22:20)

> Though I walk in the midst of dangers,
>> you guard my life when my enemies rage.
> You stretch out your hand;
>> your right hand saves me.
> The LORD is with me to the end.
>> LORD, your mercy endures forever.
>> Never forsake the work of your hands! (Ps 138:7–8)

> Listen, God, to my prayer;
>> do not hide from my pleading;
>> hear me and give answer.

> I rock with grief; I groan
> > at the uproar of the enemy,
> > the clamor of the wicked. (Ps 55:2–4)

> You are my shelter; you guard me from distress;
> > with joyful shouts of deliverance you surround me.
> > (Ps 32:7)

As Tom becomes more familiar with various Scripture passages, the Holy Spirit becomes his teacher. We also see the face of Christ when we pray, when we read Sacred Scripture, when we perform acts of charity, when we practice the corporal and spiritual works of mercy, and when we forgive. All of these moments of grace help us to live the life of virtue. One of the most important lessons we learn is the primary importance of humility. In the life of purity, one either humbles himself or herself or is humiliated.

THE ACTION OF THE HOLY SPIRIT

The pain of failure can be an important moment. An important time of healing can be hidden within the frustration. The strength to live the moral life does not rest with, or even begin with, our good intentions and resolutions alone. The Church teaches that our strength to live the moral life does not come primarily from our own efforts. Our strength comes from the Holy Spirit. The Holy Spirit is the Third Person of the Blessed Trinity. He is the bond and fruit of the love between the Father and the Son. Our (often repeated!) first steps to conversion must begin with the action of the Holy Spirit. He eternally seals and eternally expresses the fruitful gift of love between God the Father and God the Son.[3] Well, what he does in the Trinity from all eternity, is also his mission in time and space: His mission is to bring the eternal love of the Trinity into time. He does this in the creation of the world; He does this when the Eternal Son of God is made incarnate in the womb of the Blessed Virgin Mary; He does this at the redemption on the cross; He does this for the Church; He does this by sharing his life with the members of the Church. He does this when we receive the Sacraments. Pope Benedict XVI points out that in Jesus' conversation with the Samaritan woman, water is a symbol of the Holy Spirit.[4] The Holy Spirit *does something* when we go to confession and when we receive the Eucharist. Every time we pray he trains us and shows us the way to be a gift of self through love even in the ups and downs, the ins and outs of life. The Holy Spirit literally creates an impulse, a new movement of love and friendship with God through bringing the life of charity to birth in our heart. We become a gift of self not simply by measuring up to all our external obligations and fulfilling the minimal measure of our duties. The Holy Spirit influences our freedom so that we are attracted to truly good things in a way that becomes more and more spontaneous. His grace leads us to actually be attracted to the authentically true and the genuine good even in the midst of temptations and trials, failures and frustrations. He turns despair into hope. He transforms us at every level of our being so that our individual free choices and actions are truly human and directed toward the true meaning of life.

Freedom is not having everything we want when we want it. This is an illusion. A lifestyle built on this is cruelly demanding, and is not freedom at all, but slavery. Instead of being devoted to authentic goodness, we slavishly follow our cravings and neglect those we are called to love. Grace and virtue free us so we do not follow the dictatorship of our cravings, but the freedom of our call—to be human and therefore live life as a free gift of self.

The Holy Spirit is always at work in us, urging us to turn to Jesus through these important paths. The Holy Spirit is not an automatic pilot in our spiritual life that makes things perfect by the wave of his hand. Rather the Holy Spirit works in us so as to lay good foundations for actually *changing* the way we think, feel, and act, so that our new, good actions are truly our own. He uses awareness, education, healing, and support as practical stepping stones to freedom from pornography. Thoughts and desires can be and are healed by the grace of God operative in and through the Church. This only happens by looking on the face of Jesus and allowing his light to guide us so that instead of being self-centered, we learn to make a gift of self.

CHAPTER 6

"I AM HE, THE ONE WHO IS SPEAKING WITH YOU" (JOHN 4:26)

LAYING THE CULTURAL FOUNDATIONS: THE IDENTITY OF THE HUMAN PERSON

In addition to the inner work involved in the battle against pornography, it is vitally important for Tom, and for us, to lay a new foundation of his worldview. The *Catechism of the Catholic Church* teaches that, "Chastity represents an eminently personal task; it also involves a cultural effort...."[1] The use of pornography is exacerbated by a misunderstanding about the identity of the human person. Most likely, Tom is caught up in the dominant worldview and mindset of the contemporary culture that understands the human person as one who is entitled to acquire pleasure at every instance, rather than to understand *the person as a gift*. In chapters 1 to 5, Tom learned the grace of Jesus forms the believer to discover how to live as an authentic gift of self in the life of virtue. At the same time, it is crucial Tom see the manner in which the secular culture affected him. As Tom's inner work progresses, he must have the opportunity to examine his own general understanding of the identity, meaning, and vocations of the human person and to correct the misunderstandings absorbed from the society around him.

Tom and his generation have been assaulted with ideas about the human person that are inadequate and distorted, and these ideas keep Tom imprisoned in his own cravings. These insufficient ideas erode respect for the human person, the understanding of the meaning of the human body, and the sanctity of human sexuality.

Laying the foundations means detecting how Tom views his identity as a human person created in the image and likeness of God. Tom, like us, must reflect on the questions: "What is your identity?" "Who are you?" "What does it mean to be a human person?" Reflect on that question now. Go inside and drill down. What does it mean that you are a human person?

Usually, our first responses to the question of our identity are familiar and predictable. Many of us think first of our nationality. "I am Italian." "I am Irish." "I am German." "I am Latino." "I am Asian." Who are we? As we peel back that layer, we drill deeper and often, we associate ourselves with our occupation. The 'I am what I do' functionalism creeps in. "I am in sales." "I am an office worker." "I am a laborer." "I am white collar….or blue collar." "I am an executive…I travel a lot."

Drill deeper. As we drill past our job, we focus on our education or net worth: "I am the letters after my name…or before my name." "I am my grades…my degree… I am that envelope at the end of the month…I am my debt…I am my credit score." Notice that for a time in our life, we experience the odd, yet common, tendency to equate ourselves with a number. But now go beyond that, and peel it all back. Some people go to the worst experience they have had in their life and live as though the pain from this moment is their identity. Some go to the best experience they have had in their life and live from that entitlement.

Now go still deeper. Who are you? Who am I? What does it mean to be a human person? This fundamental question is our response to everything in our life.

There is a professor at an Ivy League university who holds a chair of ethics, and he maintains the proposition that a healthy chimpanzee has more of a right to life than a sick child does. Tragedy results when we make mistakes about the identity of the human being. What you say about the identity of the human being has a lot to do with how you may treat a human person. In Holland, thirty-one percent of pediatricians suppress the life of malformed infants (even without permission of parents).[2] In Switzerland, the Supreme Court declared in February 2007 the mentally ill have a constitutional right to be eliminated.[3] Forty-one percent of the world's population lives in countries where abortion is legal. There are fifty-three million surgical abortions performed every year *annually* in the world. That is equal to the total number of civilian deaths throughout World War II. Add in the atrocity of human embryonic stem cell research: the creation of, experimentation on, and periodic destruction of "spare" embryos. From this, there spreads out war, terrorism, human trafficking, and toleration of hunger. Where has all this come from? What has led to the tremendous disregard for the inviolable dignity of human life? It comes from incorrect ideas about what it means to be human. To examine what influences our ideas about the identity of the human person we have to go back briefly into history. Let's go back almost three hundred years.

Three predominant revolutions have formed today's popular notion of what it is to be a person. The Industrial Revolution, the Sexual Revolution, and the Digital Revolution have coalesced to form a common understanding in Tom's consciousness of a notion of personhood that is made to appear wonderful, but in reality, is very often quite painful.

The Industrial Revolution began in the mid 1700s and reached into the early twentieth century. Although Tom was not alive then, the values and worldview that the Industrial Revolution sparked influenced society so completely that he was greatly affected by the worldview that emerged from these times. The Industrial Revolution saw the beginning of the assembly line and the building of factories. These new measures aimed to replace the slower, handmade process so that items could now be mass-produced in a very short time and in great numbers.

As production rose, so did profits, and the assembly line needed workers. At first, these workers were mostly men. Before this, men, as fathers and husbands, worked either on the family farm or in the family store. Perhaps they worked some other job that was rather close to home and family. Before the Industrial Revolution, fathers and husbands tended, in their day job, to be no more than 700 to 800 yards away from their wife and children. Men *interacted* with their wives and children several times during the day. All of this changed with the assembly line and the factory.

Despite positive effects of industry, the assembly line became a conveyor belt that marched the father right out of the family home. The father had to awaken in the morning long before his children. He had to leave the home very early so as to clock in on time at the factory. Once there, he had to work long hours so that more items were produced, and profits were assured. The foreman, with arms folded behind him, stood over the father with a sharp eye, lest any productivity be lost. The husband/father was now under pressure until the whistle blew to signal the end of the work day. The father was absent from the home. His family did not see him often. He left before the children were awake and came home long after the children were in bed. He had to produce more and more, to make more and more money, so that the bills and debts would be paid on time.

What did the father do in 1908 when he experienced pressure at work? Did he go to the human resources office or contact the employee assistance hotline? Did he go to a workshop or an in-service on communication and conflict resolution? Did he learn to use "I statements" and a strategy of "win-win" with his boss? No. He did not *talk it out*...so he *acted it out*. But, he did not act it out at work, where he would get fired. He acted it out *at home*. He tossed and turned at night. He couldn't sleep. He worried. He swallowed the anxiety and got ulcers. He pushed the aggravation into his veins and got high blood pressure. He was more prone to bouts of temper, and had less nurturing time for his wife and children. The pressure built: the pressure of less and less access to his family and of higher demands at work. The pressures mounted and the race was under way. And the family was always the loser. In the farming or family store setting, the son learned how to use his father's tools. In the Industrial Revolution, he learned he had better avoid his father's temper. The Industrial Revolution brought the father's temper home.

And what emerged? The popular notion of the person in society became "I am what I *acquire*"—whether I acquired money, grades, fashion, the shiny car, the promotion, the bonus, the academy jacket, status, or reputation. If I acquire more hours, I acquire more money. I am what I consume. Anything that gets in the way of this becomes a target and must be eliminated. And we eliminate things by way of ideology: consumerism. Even today, we live by the notion that unless I am making some money and acquiring something out of every effort, I am simply a loser. We don't necessarily think this in the front of our minds. It lives deeper, in the back of our minds, and is therefore more present and pervasive. No wonder so many people "run" their families as if they were running a business. The pressure to make more and have more, often at the expense of family life, seeped in and formed every generation since. The irony is that no matter how much we acquire, it will never make us happy. And so, in the pain of all these attempts to acquire, men turn to satisfy their cravings, find relief, and dull the pain of insecurity through a quick fix of excessive drinking, gambling, shopping, overeating, or sexualizing, especially through cybersex—all with devastating effects on the person, marriage, family, and society.

To return to history: Around the turn of the century, when the Industrial Revolution had perfected its assault on the family, and most often the men, the Sexual Revolution came on the scene. Now that fathers had been separated from the home, the target moved deeper into the home against the mother and the child. Margaret Sanger's campaign against larger families was essentially an attack against the child. Sanger attacked the life-giving purpose of sexual love between husband and wife. She took the child out of the sexual relationship. Sigmund Freud, meanwhile, by emphasizing pansexualism, led the popular mind to believe that we could not live without sex. For Freud, sex was the energy and power behind even the most fundamental experiences and attitudes of the human person. The influence of Freud's thought was to downplay the child and exalt pleasure.

The Sexual Revolution started in earnest in the 1950s with the discovery of the hormonal nature of the phasic cycle of the female reproductive system. Before the Sexual Revolution, the nature boundary of the possibility of pregnancy tended to keep promiscuity in check. Contraception consisted of withdrawal or barrier methods, both of which were understood by the public at large to be wrong. The longstanding values of the sanctity of human sexuality began to erode at considerable pace. Already in 1948, Dorothy Day wrote that the Church's doctrine on sex and marriage was the most neglected of her teaching, even more neglected than the teachings on social justice.[4]

With the production of synthetic hormones, the anovulent pill was born. The contraceptive pill fueled the attack on human sexuality. It was argued that because men did not have to deal with the consequences of promiscuity and casual sex, especially a possible pregnancy, men had more sexual "freedom." The barrier and withdrawal methods of contraception interfered with pleasure and were not always dependable in their "success" of avoiding pregnancy. The Pill was presented as preventing pregnancy with a higher "success rate" than other methods, while being under the complete control of the woman. She did not have to depend on the man at all for this method. It was promised that women would now be on the same sexual footing as men: They would not have to have to deal with any of the "consequences," especially pregnancy, of casual, promiscuous sex. But these "promises" were revealed as false.

The contraceptive pill had devastating effects. Contraception separates the inherent connection between unitive meaning and procreative meaning of the conjugal marital act. The deliberate separation of life and love one from the other turns the self-giving conjugal act into a self-taking, contraceptive act, regardless of the intention or circumstance. The nature of love is life, and the nature of life is love. Contraception utters a loud "no" in the midst of what can only be a "yes." To deliberately separate life and love harms both the life-giving and love-giving meanings of marriage. The Pill, as with all contraception, also has a kind of extended-release effect that seeps into and permeates every relational level of the married couple. The separation of love and life in the conjugal act is the nucleus of further separations on every level of the married couple's life: They separate life and love in their discussions, plans, behavior, hopes, dreams, and attitudes. In the Sexual Revolution, the emphasis in making decisions was not long on, "Is this right or wrong?" but, "Will this make me feel good or not?"

The contraceptive pill led not to equality, but to more promiscuity. Pope Paul VI foretold that if the contraceptive pill was mainstreamed, there would be devastating consequences and effects. First, there would be an increase in marital infidelity. Second, there would be a general lowering of moral standards, especially among the young. Third, there would be a lack of reverence for women, with men treating women as mere instruments of pleasure. And fourth, public authorities would attempt to impose contraception on their people.[5] Tragically, all of these consequences came to pass. The prophecy of Pope Paul VI was not a random premonition or a guess. It was simple logic: To deliberately separate the unity between life and love harms both, and topples the first domino in a long series, kicking off a chain reaction that forecloses on the family in short order.

The first victim of promiscuity is always the woman. The Pill did not make women "equal" to men. Instead, with its "promise" to prevent pregnancy, men felt less hesitant to engage in promiscuous sex. With an increase in promiscuity under the banner of "casual" or "recreational" sex came a rise in adultery; with adultery came more divorce; and with an increase in divorce came "no fault" divorce and fatherlessness. The widespread acceptance of pornography as industry and as recreation is a direct effect of the promiscuity advanced by the Sexual Revolution.

It is ironic that as marriage was the bane of the first wave of the Sexual Revolution, it has now become the prize in the latest wave of that same revolution in the call for same-sex "marriage." In the first wave, the call was that no one be married. The commitment to the bond of marriage would inhibit so-called "sexual freedom." Thirty years later, the call is that everyone should be married and anything should be marriage.

The Sexual Revolution and its accent on free love, no-fault divorce, contraception, and promiscuity attempted to discount the inherent connection between sex and love, and between love and marriage. The emphasis shifted to sex being simply about pleasure. The notion of personhood inherited from the Industrial Revolution shifted from "To be a person, I must acquire" to "To be a person, I must acquire *pleasure*." The Pill is the "acquire pleasure quickly" worldview achieved through a chemical compound. Its overriding effect, the separation of life and love, fosters immunity to unity and self-gift.

The third wave of the perfect storm swept through twenty to thirty years later with the start of the still-ongoing Digital Revolution. In the 1980s and 1990s, technology went from the television to the video game and then the computer. The video game was the midpoint between the TV and the computer screen. Then followed the cell phone, the iPod, streaming video, social networking, chat rooms, and the list goes on. The Digital Revolution took us on to the Information Superhighway. Information and entertainment were available at the click of a button. The computer provides instant access to whatever we seem to crave: the Internet is available in the bedroom, office, kitchen, or on the cell phone. We relate to one another only through a screen that filters our identity. Even our relationships are electronic.

We hate to wait. Why? Because we rarely have to wait anymore. We want the driver in front of us to respond to our every thought with the speed of our computer modem. The Digital Revolution invented road rage. Picture the line of traffic on a four-lane highway. The traffic light is red. The cars in the left-hand turn lane wait for the green arrow. The very moment it turns green, the driver in the twenty-fifth car in line slams his hand onto the horn, practically pushing through to the engine block! And then the orchestra starts, and it is off to the races! Horse-drawn carriages and Model T Fords did not lend themselves to road rage. Even growing up in the 1970s, I cannot recall incidents of road rage. We had a green station wagon parked at our curb; sometimes it even worked! I was the youngest of five children. We would go on long trips, and when the traffic jammed up my father would tell us a story. To this day, I can't get agitated in a traffic jam.

At the grocery store, the neon sign at the express checkout lane flashes "fifteen items or less." If we have to wait a moment too long when we stand in that lane, what do we do? We look down and we count! We count the number of items the shopper in front of us has placed on the conveyor belt. We are upset if we count more than fifteen items. And as we count, the oddest sorts of questions arise: Does a six-pack of soda count as six items or one? If there is a bunch of bananas and one became detached in the cart, is that now two items or one? We become lawyers in the checkout line! Why? Because we are accustomed to a fast pace. The quicker our computer, the less patient our heart. We expect the person in front of us in line to be quick…as quick, in fact, as our modem—to respond to our impulses within two and a half seconds! If other people do not move quickly enough, we start to make judgments about their IQ! We hate to wait: at the ATM, at the post office, or for the traffic signal to change. The notion from the Industrial and Sexual Revolutions that "to be a person I must acquire pleasure" morphs into, with the Digital Revolution, "to be a person I must acquire pleasure *quickly*." If I do not acquire pleasure quickly, I am somehow a failure. What we have inherited from the Digital Revolution is that to be a person, not only must I *acquire pleasure,* but I must *acquire pleasure quickly*…otherwise I really do not count…I am a loser. Unless my life looks like the lives of the people in the pictures of *People* magazine, somehow I am not a person. And so we escape into fantasy and unreality: "If only I had the looks, the trust fund, and the ability of the popular scholar-athlete." This notion of personhood only increases self-centeredness at every level: education, occupation, relationships, marriage, family, and recreation. This mistaken notion of the person has been nourished for more than two generations. "*Acquire pleasure quickly*" is the dominant and prevalent understanding of what it is to be a person. It strips the gears of the true meaning of personhood and it wreaks havoc on the person, marriage, and family.

At least two generations have been formed to really believe that to be human means to *acquire pleasure quickly*. This is the DNA code, the genome, for the ideologies of the culture of death such as individualism, entitlement, hedonism (pleasure), utilitarianism, consumerism, and materialism. No matter how much we chase after it, we cannot change the basic effect of money: the more you get, the more you want, the *less* it satisfies. The notion of acquiring pleasure quickly shapes, or rather, *mis-shapes* the human conscience and blurs the sense of personhood.

Acquire pleasure quickly is the game plan of the advertising industry. It is the strategy of the entertainment world. The entertainment industry exploits the powerful urges and feelings associated with the sexual drive, and leads young people to believe that sexuality is only for the satisfaction of personal erotic need. Many adults find themselves burdened with indulgent patterns that have been developed and reinforced from an early age. Now, they feel embarrassed at their behavior and actions. They feel desperate, as if there is no way out.

What is the proper understanding of the identity of the human person? Who are we deep down? A reflection may illustrate. I was born in August 1967. This means that my mother and father came together in an act of love sometime in late November, early December 1966. In that act of love, they shared everything they were: their full identity, emotions, pains, blessings, histories, genetics, and more; all of this was shared along a biological, physiological, and sexual matrix by which my father made a total gift of self in love to my mother. In receiving his gift, she made a gift in love to him of all she was. And I am the result. I am the love of my parents. That act of love in which they engaged in late in 1966 has never ended. I am a gift of love, not a trophy to be acquired. Therefore, the only thing that can fulfill me is to be a gift of love. I can only find myself through the sincere gift of self.[6]

THE THEOLOGY OF THE BODY

Tom must be presented with and hear a new understanding of his identity that effectively counters the "acquire pleasure quickly" notion of personhood. The theology of the body in the teaching of Blessed Pope John Paul II does just this. His teaching on the human person and marriage is like the discovery of a long-lost scroll, its contents all but forgotten. The theology of the body proclaims the inviolable dignity of the human and the meaning and beauty of marriage and human sexuality as the gift of self.

In October 1978, a rare and unmistakable presence came to the world stage. Karol Wojtyla, the newly elected pope who had chosen the name John Paul II, had experienced not one, but two of the most terrifying totalitarian regimes in history. As a son of Poland, he experienced the onslaught of Nazism and soon after, the savage effects of Soviet Communism in his homeland. His first defense against both of these regimes was to turn to the inviolable dignity of the human person, and to the sanctity of marriage and family. He would journey into the mountains of Poland with married couples. There, they would discuss the importance of married love and family life and the vital influence of both on culture and society. These discussions formed their resistance to the Nazi and later, the Soviet, regimes. The culture and life that the Nazis and Communists sought to trample upon and destroy, Karol Wojtyla held high and proclaimed loudly. He was well suited to face the third totalitarian regime, which he would respond to as pope: the regime of the dictatorship of relativism in the latter half of the twentieth century. His first call to arms was the teaching on the theology of the body.

The theology of the body is a popular expression for the teaching that John Paul II delivered to the audiences he held on Wednesdays from 1979 to 1984 (an expression that later became the title of the book when the talks were collected). The Holy

Father would greet the pilgrims who had come to Rome and also give a teaching on that day. His theme during this time was on the human person, marriage, and family. His passion for the topic was outdone only by the persistence of his teaching.

He began by talking about Jesus, and based his teaching on the discussion Jesus had with the Pharisees in the nineteenth chapter of the Gospel of St. Matthew. The Pharisees come to Jesus and ask him a question about divorce: "Is it lawful for a man to divorce his wife for any cause whatever?" (Matt 19:3). They want to trap Jesus. If he responds "yes," then they can say that he is not really serious about the depth of love to which he is calling people. If he responds, "no," then he is contradicting Moses, who allowed divorce because of the hardness of the people's hearts. Jesus responds by saying, "Have you not read that from the beginning the Creator 'made them male and female' and said, 'For this reason a man shall leave his father and mother and be joined to his wife, and the two shall become one flesh'? So they are no longer two, but one flesh. Therefore, what God has joined together, no human being must separate" (Matt 19:4–6). The Pharisees ask Jesus why Moses permitted divorce, and Jesus responds, "Because of the hardness of your hearts Moses allowed you to divorce your wives, but from the beginning it was not so" (Matt 19:8).

John Paul II notes that Jesus does not accept the question at the level at which his interlocutors attempt to introduce it. They ask, when it comes to divorce, "What may you do?" Jesus says, in effect, "If you ask me what you may or may not do, you have to go further—what is the identity of the human person? Who are you?" Thus, John Paul II points out that Jesus, on the question of divorce and marriage, appeals not once, but twice to "the beginning." Jesus is speaking about Genesis: to the creation of the human person. When Jesus answers the Pharisees, he includes two quotes from Genesis: "...the Creator 'made them male and female' and said, 'For this reason a man shall leave his father and mother and be joined to his wife, and the two shall become one flesh."' The first quote, "made them male and female," is from the first chapter of Genesis, and his second quote, "a man shall leave his father and mother and be joined to his wife, and the two shall become one flesh" is from the second chapter. This means that Jesus wants us to go to Genesis to find out about the true identity of the human person as God intended it.

Catholics can become somewhat nervous or hesitant about going to Genesis. We might feel a little embarrassed, and perhaps even apologetic. We have been led to believe that the creation stories in Genesis are myths. By this we believe that they are not true. The creation accounts of Genesis are true. They are myths in the *classic sense* of myth: They tell us a truth that is *so true* that it *cannot fit in a mere fact*. The truth of myth is a truth that is *too dense to fit in a fact*. The creation accounts in Genesis are true: They communicate to us the truth about who created us and why he created us. Science, based on observation and measurement, is simply not equipped to deal with the "who" or the "why" of our creation. Science deals with the "when" and the "how." Theology and philosophy deal with the "why" and the "who." The Creation accounts communicate to us, among other things, the truth of our identity as human persons. This is why Jesus himself refers to Genesis.

Jesus refers first to the first account of creation in Genesis: "Have you not read that from the beginning the Creator made them male and female?" This refers to the twenty-seventh verse of the first chapter of Genesis. We recall the first account of creation. This is the one that begins: "When God created the heaven and the earth…" and then proceeds with a series of commands on each of the individual days of creation. "Then God said, 'Let there be light,' and there was light…the first day." And the account continues in a crisp, day-by-day structure. God commands and the visible world arises, until the sixth day, and then all the commands stop. On the sixth day, God pauses. He draws within himself, and says, "Let us make human beings in our own image, after our likeness. Let them have dominion over the fish of the sea, the birds of the air, the tame animals, the wild animals and all the creatures that crawl on the ground" (Gen 1:26). God has not done this for any other of his creations. He did not pause to think about it before he created rocks, trees, or animals. He just created them outright, but now he pauses. It is as if he placed his hand on his chin, contemplating, and he drew within himself to seek the blueprint for the creation of man. Our identity is different from animals, vegetables, and minerals.

After contemplating the creation of the human person, God creates. He makes the breathtaking choice: "God created man in his image; in the divine image he created him; male and female he created them" (Gen 1:27). In the first account, God creates man and woman at the same time. Notice that the human person and marriage are created at the very same time, in the very same moment, in the very same breath of God. Man's identity is directly related to the gift of self as found in marriage. Man is created in the image and likeness of God.

John Paul II points out that Jesus also referred to the second account of creation. So if we are going to look for the true identity of the human person, we also have to consider the second account. The second account differs from the first account of creation. This account is more story-like. The major difference is that in this account, man and woman are not created at the same time. There is an interval of time between their creations. Man is created first (Gen 2:7). Adam is created from the mud of the clay of the earth, that which is lowest, and from the deep breath of God, that which is highest. Adam differs from the rest of creation: He has the capacity to know and to love...has a conscience, and as such, he can make the painful decision to reject God's love.

Adam is given three tasks. He must "till the soil" (Gen 2:5b), name the animals (Gen 2:19), and keep the command regarding the mysterious tree of the knowledge of good and evil (Gen 2:17). John Paul II points out that these three tasks tell us something very important about the identity of the human person. In fact, these tasks make clear a series of foundational or "original experiences" that are crucial to grasp the meaning of human personhood.

The first task, tilling the soil, reveals something to man about his identity. Through tilling the soil, man discovers he is different from the material world. He, in and through his body, can till, plant, sew, and reap. He can, through his body, his choices, and actions initiate and bring to bear a whole series of realities in the physical world...and in himself. As man interacts with the world, he learns he is the only being that has the capacity to know and to love. Rocks do not have this capacity for love. Animals have the capacity for instinct, but not for intellect and will. Only man has the capacity to be conscious of himself as aware of himself, and to know himself. Man not only knows. He can *know* that he knows. Man not only has the capacity to love. He can *love* that he loves. John Paul II refers to this as man's experience of "original solitude." The first meaning of man's solitude is not solitude in the sense of man being on a spiritual retreat...rather it is *solitude* in the sense that man has the capacity to be aware of his internal spiritual identity. John Paul II refers to this as the first meaning of the identity of the human person: That man has the capacity to know and to love. Man experiences this again when he names the animals. In and through his body, just as he did when he tilled the soil, man is aware of his difference from the animals. "None of these proved to be a suitable partner for the man" (Gen 2:20). This affirms the truth that, "It is not good for the man to be alone. I will make a suitable partner for him" (Gen 2:18). The command regarding the tree reveals that man has the capacity to influence his future through his choices and actions. If he disobeys the command, he will die. He has never done *that* before. He has never *died*. But he knows that through his own choice and action, he can bring that about. John Paul II points out man is aware he has the power of will and self-determination.

Yet, there is more to his identity. Not only does man have the capacity to be conscious of his self-awareness, self-knowledge, and self-determination, but man experiences these things as *a search outside of himself*. This is, for John Paul II, the second meaning of original solitude, and vital to the identity of the human person. Man is *in search*. In fact, John Paul II says this is most important to man's identity: Man seeks outside himself for another like himself. As we saw, above, God confirms this: "It is not good that man should be alone. I will make a suitable partner for him." It is interesting that God says that there is something "not good." There has been no sin yet. How can there be something "not good." What is really at work here is the sense that man, in his deepest identity, is not yet complete; in one sense, the act of creation is not yet finished.

John Paul II next refers to "original unity," the creation of the human person as man and woman as central to man's identity. This is found in the Genesis account; when God creates woman he places the man in a deep sleep (Gen 2: 21). This is a particular kind of sleep—it is in a sense, a prayer. In the Bible, sleep has a particular meaning. Extraordinary events take place while one is asleep, or just after one awakens. Abram, who will become Abraham, falls into a sleep or a trance prior to the tremendous vision of God (Gen 15:12). Jacob has an experience of God while sleeping (Gen 32:25). Samuel hears the voice of God while he sleeps" (1 Sam 3:1–14). The apostles fall asleep at the transfiguration during the agony in the garden (Luke 9:32; 22:45). St. Joseph, as he is sleeping, learns through a dream of the virginal conception of Jesus (Matt 1:20). Notice that the Blessed Mother, conceived without sin, learns of the plan of God directly from the angel while she is awake (Luke 1:26-38).

So too, Adam, while he sleeps, experiences the great action of God in the creation of woman. The woman is made from his rib, close to his heart. She is created from his body. They share the same humanity. On waking and seeing the woman, Adam does something he has not done yet. He has not done this when he saw the beauty of creation, of landscapes and seascape. He has not done this when he saw the animals, or the mountains: He *speaks*. For the first time, he speaks, and calls out: "This one, at last, is bone of my bones, and flesh of my flesh; this one shall be called 'woman,' for out of man' this one has been taken" (Gen 2:23). Notice the search at the basis of his identity as Adam cries out, "This one, *at last*...." The meaning of his body and hers, of his identity and hers, now fills the consciousness, self-awareness, self-knowledge, and self-determination of both of them: "The man and his wife were both naked, yet they felt no shame" (Gen 2:25). John Paul II refers to this experience as "original nakedness." It does not simply mean that they were standing there with no clothes on. Original nakedness refers to their identity. They are aware of the spousal and nuptial meaning of their own body and that of the other. In fact, the first thing Adam speaks about is the beauty of her body. Their nakedness means that nothing obstructs, nothing gets in the way of their simple, immediate, direct understanding of the meaning of their own body and that of the other. They know and understand they are meant to be a gift of self through joining in a communion of persons. In this, in their nakedness, they see the very same thing that God saw when he looked at everything he had made and "found it very good" (Gen 1:31).

THE GIFT OF SELF IN LOVE

Husband and wife in marriage make a total and complete gift of self in love, which culminates in the two-in-one flesh union. The two-in-one flesh union is an utterly unique action, rather than simply a sexual act. The persons of husband and wife truly become one in a total gift of self. This oneness is accomplished in and through the sexual difference, male-to-female and female-to-male. Husband and wife take everything they are and make a gift of self in and through the full reality of their body, one to another in an act of love: the conjugal, marital act.

In the conjugal act, the husband gives everything he is: his history, genetics, emotions, mind, heart, and soul to his wife in love. In this same conjugal act, his wife receives everything he is, and in this receiving she shares with him all she is: her history, genetics, emotions, mind, heart, and soul, in love. In this self-gift of love, at its height, when they have given themselves in love to such a degree that they are outside themselves in the excitement of love, it is then that life is possible. This act reveals the profound meaning of the body, sexuality, and sexual difference. The basic biological and physiological realities are integral to the personal identity of man and woman. New life can emerge directly from this moment of love. Man has no right to separate life from this moment of love. The conjugal act proves beyond all doubt that the nature of life is love...and that the nature of love is life. To separate life and love at this moment injures the civilization of love and harms the culture of life. Pornography encourages and advances this separation. The love between husband and wife leads them in the moment of the conjugal act to overflow and become *ek-static* (from the Greek ekstasis, meaning astonishment, or outside oneself in wonder): outside themselves in love—they have *become a gift of self* on every level of their being, including the physical and sexual. Such a gift is, of its very nature, permanent, faithful, and open to life.

The worldview of "acquire pleasure quickly" is subtle, fine-grained, and rampant in movies, advertising, and magazines. It is temptation's fuel. Its toxic residue, like secondhand smoke, filters in and affects even people of good will. It affects even practicing Catholics. "Acquire pleasure quickly" first obscures the self-gift of marriage and family, presenting each as an unreachable ideal, simply a fairy tale. "Acquire pleasure quickly" simply cannot fit with vows of marriage, because the vows are not acquired, they are not always pleasurable, and they take time. "Acquire pleasure quickly" encourages impulsivity, entitlement, deception, lies, betrayal, double-talk, duplicity, illusions, and using others until nothing is left over. It induces good men like Tom to drift away from marriage and family into Internet pornography. "Acquire pleasure quickly" is slavery. Although slavery wears many disguises, it always seeks to portray itself as freedom. Internet pornography always winds its way into slavery; it takes many forms and claims many victims. Behind its seemingly dazzling and alluring disguise, there is only emptiness. The emptiness is like a black hole that consumes marriage and family, the dignity of the human person and the sanctity of human sexuality. Tom, and many good men, fall into this hole. At the urging of a temptation they embark on the "acquire pleasure quickly" path. After all, "everyone is doing it."

The first few miles seemed to be filled with thrills and pay-offs. "Acquire pleasure quickly" seemed to be the law of the land; its promise of fitting in has actually turned out to be a life sentence with no parole in sight. Tom's unease was there all along, just beneath the surface. Now, after the bottom falls out, they look back over the map of the last few years. They now see all the self-constructed roadblocks, lost opportunities, lack of a future, and loss of good name. They see only two turns remaining on this road: One leads to a cliff, the other to a dead end—a crossroads if ever there was one: to the one side divorce and debt, and to the other loss of job and future. But there is an overgrown path, barely visible, obscured by years of neglect, and even if they see it, it is uphill all the way, exhausting for sure. Yet, the path has a unique character because it grows more visible the more one seeks it. And on top there appears to be what looks like an anchor, and also like a cross. Tom can see the footprints of the one who has led the way up this hill. Turning onto this path means the thorns of suffering. It means saying "no" to self and "yes" to the gift. Every no is built on a deeper yes. This is the path of mercy, that of the gift of self. The moment one steps toward this path, one becomes a pilgrim.

The teaching of John Paul II is a shaft of light aimed at making clear that the identity of the human person is always and everywhere to be a gift of self. This is the center of the renewal of a culture of marriage. The theology of the body dips into the marrow of the faith and shows us that the person is created not to *acquire*, but to be a *gift*; the person is not created to acquire *pleasure*, but to give *beauty*; the person is created not to acquire pleasure *quickly*, but to give beauty *slowly*, *contemplatively*, with the precision of a lover. This understanding of creation lays the foundation for purity of heart.

John Paul II next describes original shame. In the third chapter of Genesis, Satan approaches Eve and tempts her to disobey God's command, to eat of the tree of the knowledge of good and evil. She gives into the devil's temptation, as does Adam. At this moment, when they disobey God, John Paul II points out that, out of fear, they question the gift in their heart, and through their deliberate choice and action cast God from their heart. They realize they are naked (Gen 3:7), cover their bodies in the sign of the relation one to another, and hide. Original shame affects them at the deepest level of their being. They lose the experience of the gift, experience alienation instead, and seek to dominate and possess the other, rather than be a gift of self. There is now a fracture, a fundamental loss, a deformation that overturns their search in love for the other. Where before there had been love, there is now resistance. Yet, John Paul II points out that God, through the redemption wrought by Jesus, the Son of God, through his self-gift on the cross, man receives the strength of grace to heal him, save him from sin and give him the strength to live the life of virtue. This strength is life in the Holy Spirit. Pope John Paul II emphasizes that the Holy Spirit calls each of us to the grace of Jesus, which is derived from his self-gift of love on the cross for his bride, the Church. We are not only called, but we are called, as John Paul II teaches, with *effectiveness* by the Holy Spirit to rediscover the spousal meaning of the body, wounded by sin, but healed by grace and strengthened by virtue.

TEMPERANCE

Temperance is the virtue that helps the Christian to interiorize the call to holiness as regards the instinct for pleasure. Temperance is not a prudish denial of sexuality, but a deep and wonderful acknowledgement of its true meaning. As noted previously, John Paul II teaches purity is a hidden spring.[7] The Holy Spirit longs to lead us to this spring. We begin to discover this wonderful fountain when we say "no" to Internet pornography, and do so for a deeper and more profound "yes"…the "yes" to the gift of self. John Paul II describes chastity as a hidden wellspring, the source of which is in the interior of man, in his heart.[8] The Pontifical Biblical Commission in *The Bible and Morality: Biblical Roots of Christian Conduct* uses the same image: "The well-spring of Christian morality is not an external norm but the experience of God's love for every individual…."[9] Jesus forms the Samaritan woman with his words: "Whoever drinks the water that I shall give will never thirst; the water that I shall give will become in him a spring of water welling up to eternal life" (John 4:14). This is similar, too, to the later words of Jesus in the Gospel:

"'Whoever believes in me, as Scripture says, 'Rivers of living water will flow from within him'" (John 7:38). This living water is the action of the Holy Spirit that forms the life of virtue in the believer. Purity and temperance are not programmed into us automatically. They are virtues that are instilled in us over time, which are assisted by the other virtues. The virtues assist us to do good and avoid evil.[10] New growth is always fragile. Tom may fail many times, and so might we. We may relapse and grow frustrated. Even here, God has not given up on us. The Holy Spirit is eager to forgive us through the sacramental ministry of the Church, and to lead us again to the hidden wellspring.

CONCLUSION

When the Holy Spirit teaches us, our heart opens to Jesus just as the heart of the Samaritan woman opened to him. It was necessary that Jesus met this woman. At first, she resisted him and lashes out: "How can you, a Jew, ask me, a Samaritan woman, for a drink?" (Luke 4:9). She appeals to prejudice and defensiveness to isolate herself in her pain. But through his gift of self, she grows in her awareness of the identity of Jesus: "Sir, you do not even have a bucket and the cistern is deep; where then can you get this living water?" (Luke 4:11). Her reference to him with the polite and generic address "Sir" demonstrates that she is growing in her awareness of the identity of Jesus. After receiving the self-gift of Jesus, which includes his naming her sin and forgiving it, she proclaims to the town: "Come see a man who told me everything I have done. Could he possibly be the Messiah?" And they said to the woman, "We no longer believe because of your word; for we have heard for ourselves, and we know that this is truly the savior of the world" (Luke 4:29, 42). Notice that while before she hid in fear away from the patterns of the community, after meeting Jesus she makes a gift of self to the community.

As we said at the beginning of these pages, there are no magical solutions to life. There are only living solutions to life. God does not send us self-help books, techniques, or systems. He sends us his Son. The Son of God has taken upon himself all of our suffering, pain, and sin. In return, he gives us his living water of grace. For the Samaritan woman, the gift of Jesus has transformed her fear into the gift of authentic love. He longs to do the same for all who are affected by Internet pornography.

Our docility and trust to the invitation of Jesus to the healing life of grace and virtue is the beautiful inner work to which God invites us. This is the call to holiness and the summons of the new evangelization. Similar to that of the Samaritan woman, the journey is not painless or without its challenges. But Jesus, as he did with the Samaritan woman, promises to accompany us. He does not promise us that the journey will be easy, but does promise he will love us on the journey.

We may be in the intense heat of the day. We may be suffering from the effects of Internet pornography and cybersex. We may be embarrassed, burdened, confused, and suffering. We may be tired of the secrets and thirsty for the truth. The well is not too far away, and in fact, there is someone sitting by it. He is the very profile of beauty itself. He turns and offers us a gift. It is his gift of self, and he invites us to receive a new measure from the wellspring of his love.

NOTES

INTRODUCTION

1. The patristic scholar Cardinal Jean Daniélou, SJ, explains the temptation to magic was the first of all temptations. See his *The Scandal of Truth* (London: Burns and Oates, 1962), 54.

CHAPTER 1

1. What follows immediately is a fictitious account. The names and circumstances are not based on an actual situation, and have no relation or basis in fact or history, but are presented to give an example of the manner in which the phenomenon of Internet pornography can occur almost undetected. Here, *pornography* is meant to refer exclusively to adult pornography. It in no way refers to child pornography, which is a criminal offense and for which the proper civil law enforcement authorities must be notified immediately.

2. See Patrick Carnes, PhD, David L. Delmonico, PhD, Elizabeth Griffin, MA, with Joseph Moriarity, *In the Shadows of the Net: Breaking Free of Compulsive Online Sexual Behavior* (Center City, MN: Hazelden, 2001), 7.

3. Ibid., 6.

4. See Pamela Paul, "From Pornography to Porno to Porn: How Porn Became the Norm," *The Social Costs of Pornography* (Princeton, NJ: The Witherspoon Institute, 2010), 4.

5. See Carnes, Delmonico, and Griffin, 6.

CHAPTER 2

1. See Warwick Neville, "Old Testament Spousal Narratives: A Contribution to the 'Nuptial Mystery,'" *Dialoghi Sul Mistero Nuziale*, eds. G. Marengo and B. Ognibeni (Rome: Lateran University Press, 2003), 185–204.

2. St. Bonaventure, *Commentary on the Gospel of Luke as in Works of St. Bonaventure*, ed., Robert J. Karris, OFM (St. Bonaventure, NY: Franciscan Institute Publications, 2003), 1545.

CHAPTER 3

1. CCC, no. 2354.

2. See the discussion of happiness in Jean Daniélou, *The Scandal of Truth* (London: Burns and Oates, 1962), 44–47.

3. Pope John Paul II, *Man and Woman He Created Them: A Theology of the Body*, ed. Michael Waldstein. (Boston: Pauline Books and Media, 2006).

4. United States Conference of Catholic Bishops, *Happy Are Those Who Are Called to His Supper: On Preparing to Receive Christ Worthily in the Eucharist* (December 2006), 4.

5. Pontifical Council for Social Communications, *Pornography and Violence in the Communications Media: A Pastoral Response* (1989), 17.

6. Karol Wojtyla, *Love and Responsibility* (San Francisco: Ignatius Press, 1993), 192–93.

7. See the neurological effects of addiction in Gerald G. May, MD, *Addiction and Grace* (San Francisco: Harper and Row, 1988), 64 ff. See also Kevin Skinner, *Treating Pornography Addiction: The Essential Tools for Recovery* (Provo, UT: Growth Climate Inc., 2005), 45–55.

8. *The Social Costs of Pornography: A Statement of Findings and Recommendations* (Princeton, NJ: The Witherspoon Institute, 2010), 17.

9. A. Cooper, et al., "Cyber Sex Users and Abusers and Compulsives: New Findings and Implications," in *Cybersex: The Dark Side of the Net*, a special issue of the journal *Sexual Addiction and Compulsivity*, ed. Al Cooper (New York: Routledge, 2000), 6. See also Carnes, Delmonico, Griffin, *In the Shadows of the Net*, 12–14.

10. J. Suler, "The Online Disinhibition Effect," *CyberPsychology and Behavior* 7 (2004), 321–26.

11. See Carnes, Delmonico, Griffin, *In the Shadows of the Net*, 44–49.

12. For an explanation of the cycle, see Cardinal Justin Rigali, *Let the Oppressed Go Free: Breaking the Bonds of Addiction* (Dallas, TX: Basilica Press, 2009), 27–30.

13. "Pornography's Impact on Marriage and the Family," testimony of Jill C. Manning before the Subcommittee on the Constitution, Civil Rights and Property Rights, Committee on Judiciary, United States Senate, Nov. 9, 2005.

14. Pamela Paul, "From Pornography to Porno to Porn: How Porn Became the Norm," *The Social Costs of Pornography* (Princeton, NJ: The Witherspoon Institute, 2010), 12.

15. See The Witherspoon Institute, *The Social Costs of Pornography*, 24, 40.

16. See Second Vatican Council, *Gaudium et Spes* 50.

CHAPTER 4

1. The following scenarios are fictitious accounts. The names and circumstances are not based in any actual situation, and have no relation or basis in fact or history.

2. See Bruno Forte, *To Follow You, Light of Life: Spiritual Exercises Preached Before John Paul II at the Vatican* (Grand Rapids, MI: Eerdmans, 2005), 33.

3. St. Ambrose, *Explanation of the Gospel*, PL 15, col. 1633, Book IV in Luke, pars. 68–79.

4. CCC, no. 2352.

5. See Romanus Cessario, OP, "Sacramental Confession and Addictions," in *Addiction and Compulsive Behaviors: Proceeding of the 17th Workshop for Bishops,* ed. Edward J. Furton (Boston: The National Catholic Bioethics Center, 2000), 125–39, esp. 130.

6. Apostolic Journey of His Holiness Benedict XVI to Brazil on the Occasion of the Fifth General Conference of the Bishops of Latin America and the Caribbean, Meeting with the Community Living in

the Fazenda, Greeting of His Holiness Benedict XVI, Fazenda da Esperança, Guaratinguetá, May 12, 2007.

7. See Pope John Paul II, *Rich in Mercy*, 7.

8. See John Paul II, *Man and Woman He Created Them: A Theology of the Body*, ed. Michael Waldstein (Boston: Pauline Books and Media, 2006), 282–84.

9. Cardinal Justin Rigali, *Let the Oppressed Go Free: Breaking the Bonds of Addiction* (Dallas: Basilica Press, 2009), 73.

10. Norman Doidge, "Acquiring Tastes and Loves," *The Social Costs of Pornography* (Princeton, NJ: The Witherspoon Institute, 2010), 43–44.

11. Kevin Skinner, *Treating Pornography Addiction: The Essential Tools for Recovery* (Provo, UT: Growth Climate Inc., 2005), 103–6.

12. CCC, no. 2342.

CHAPTER 5

1. *Gaudium et Spes*, 24.

2. For the significance of the use of short Scripture verses in the spiritual life, see Evagrius Ponticus, *Talking Back: Antirrhêtikos* trans. David Brakke (Collegeville, MN: The Liturgical Press, 2009), introduction 14–30. See also Douglas Burton-Christie, *The Word in the Desert: Scripture and the Quest for Holiness in Early Christian Monasticism* (New York: Oxford University Press, 1993), 107–29.

3. St. Thomas Aquinas, *Summa Contra Gentiles* IV, 20–21, esp. n. 3576.

4. Pope Benedict XVI, *Jesus of Nazareth* (New York: Doubleday, 2007), 241.

CHAPTER 6

1. CCC, no. 2344.

2. Olimpia Tarzia, "Introduction, Contemporary Issues and Cultural Trends," Pontifical Council for the Laity, *Woman and Man: The* Humanum *in its Entirety On the Twentieth Anniversary of John Paul II's* Mulieris Dignitatem *(1988–2008)*, International Congress, Rome, Feb. 7–9, 2008 (Rome: Libreria Editrice Vaticana), 262.

3. Ibid., 262.

4. Dorothy Day, *On Pilgrimage* (Grand Rapids, MI: Eerdmans, 1999), 133.

5. Pope Paul VI, *Humanae Vitae* 17.

6. Cf. *Gaudium et Spes* 24.

7. See Pope John Paul II, *Man and Woman He Created Them: A Theology of the Body,* trans. Michael Waldstein (Boston: Pauline Books and Media, 2006), 320, 326.

8. Ibid., 320, 326, 328.

9. Pontifical Biblical Commission, *The Bible and Morality: Biblical Roots of Christian Conduct* (Rome: Libreria Editrice Vaticana, 2008), 55.

10. St. Thomas Aquinas, *Summa Theologica*, Ia IIae q. 94, a. 2.